BIG VISION,
SMALL BUSINESS

BIG VISION, SMALL BUSINESS

4 Keys

to Success

without

Growing Big

JAMIE S. WALTERS

BK

BERRETT-KOEHLER PUBLISHERS, INC.
San Francisco

Berrett-Koehler Publishers, Inc.
235 Montgomery Street, Suite 650
San Francisco, CA 94104-2916
Tel: (415) 288-0260   Fax: (415) 362-2512   www.bkconnection.com

ORDERING INFORMATION
Quantity sales. Special discounts are available on quantity purchases by corporations, associations, and others. For details, contact the "Special Sales Department" at the Berrett-Koehler address above.

Individual sales. Berrett-Koehler publications are available through most bookstores. They can also be ordered direct from Berrett-Koehler: Tel: (800) 929-2929; Fax: (802) 864-7626; www.bkconnection.com

Orders for college textbook/course adoption use. Please contact Berrett-Koehler: Tel: (800) 929-2929; Fax: (802) 864-7626.

Orders by U.S. trade bookstores and wholesalers. Please contact Publishers Group West, 1700 Fourth Street, Berkeley, CA 94710. Tel: (510) 528-1444; Fax (510) 528-3444.

Berrett-Koehler and the BK logo are registered trademarks of Berrett-Koehler Publishers, Inc.

Production Management: Michael Bass & Associates

Text and Cover Design: Shelby Designs and Illustrates

Printed in the United States of America

Berrett-Koehler books are printed on long-lasting acid-free paper. When it is available, we choose paper that has been manufactured by environmentally responsible processes. These may include using trees grown in sustainable forests, incorporating recycled paper, minimizing chlorine in bleaching, or recycling the energy produced at the paper mill.

Library of Congress Cataloging-in-Publication Data
Walters, Jamie S., 1963–
    Big vision, small business: four keys to success without growing big /
Jamie S. Walters.—Rev. ed.
       p.   cm.
    Includes bibliographical references and index.
    ISBN 1-57675-188-0 (pbk.)
       1. Small business—United States. 2. Small business—United States—
    Management. 3. Success in business—United States. I. Title.
HD2346.U5 W35 2002
       658.02´2—dc21   2002021562

Revised Edition
07 06 05 04 03 02   10 9 8 7 6 5 4 3 2 1

In loving memory of

Helen Elizabeth McGuire Walters

(May 4, 1908–August 1, 2000)

WHOSE LIFE AND MEMORY PROVIDE
ME WITH AN ENDURING EXAMPLE OF
RIGHT SPEECH, DEEP FAITH,
AND SELFLESS SERVICE

Contents

Preface

THE GREAT POWER OF SMALL ENTERPRISE

SMALL BUSINESSES, particularly the smallest ones, don't get the recognition and respect they deserve in our mass media–oriented culture, which primarily celebrates and worships as successful the grotesquely big—big size, big numbers, big egos, big kill. An odd reality, when you consider that 80 percent of all businesses in the United States have fewer than five employees.[1] Yet some visionary small-enterprise owners fully embrace the advantages of small size and adopt practices to hone these assets just as a master craftsman develops his or her skills. Such business owners' journeys thus become ones of qualitative depth rather than quantitative expansion.

In a culture that associates success too often with fast-growth, high-revenue, large-scale corporations, how do owners of these underappreciated small enterprises manage the many challenges of creating as well as sustaining their businesses? What inspires them to persevere with their small organizations in a world in which people are branded as unimportant, unambitious, or worse, failures, if they're not obsessed with quickly building a big company, amassing great financial wealth, and becoming the next Bill Gates? What motivates them as they struggle not just to make ends meet but to rise above mediocrity, while bombarded with news of the multimillion-dollar salaries paid to celebrity CEOs, movie stars, and athletes? What helps them keep perspective when they hear of the significant resources extended by banks and governments to help save bankrupt corporations? What makes their preference of small-scale, qualitative entrepreneurship worthwhile? What makes them strive toward greater idealism in their vision and refinement of their business relationships, thus distinguishing themselves from the "pack"?

These and other questions inspired me to write this book as one way of celebrating small enterprise—big-vision small enterprise in particular—and challenging a major assumption: that quantitative growth is the only path to satisfaction and success. I'm happy to report that this assumption is far from true, as this book will help reveal.

In writing *Big Vision, Small Business*, I wanted to share real-world information about what it's like to be a small-business owner: you'll find stories, anecdotes, profiles, ideas, and insights from actual big-vision small business owners. I also explore some of the options available to the business owner who doesn't wish to be held captive by a narrow, quantitative definition of success, so you won't see many references to a company's revenues and payroll size, nor an owner's net worth. None of those are considered reliable measures of success in this book. Indeed, *Big Vision, Small Business* emphasizes that growth and success can and should be defined qualitatively, based on, among other things, a small-enterprise owner's vision, values, lifestyle goals, and the quality of his or her relationships and contributions within and beyond the walls of the business. Growth and success become more about the quality of the journey, the lessons learned and applied, and the positive contributions in service to others, rather than a simple, raw dollar amount that means little unless you look beneath the surface.

In addition to suggesting alternatives to the prevailing quantitative definition of growth and success and paying homage to my fellow small-business owners, I hope this book provides validation for those current and prospective entrepreneurs who endeavor to rise above the norm, above the mediocre, above the minimum that is expected, by plumbing the depths of what's possible and bringing their dreams to life in ways that serve, surprise, and lift others up. If Pareto's 80-20 rule applies to small business, big-vision small-business owners are those 20 percent that set new standards and create new ways of working and being. Many people have told me that this big-vision spirit is needed more than ever in our "post-9/11" reality.

I also hope *Big Vision* serves as a resource in which people will find inspiration: new ways to think about their enterprises and their own journeys as small-business owners, a few thought-provoking ideas, and a sense of satisfaction in knowing they're part of a wonderful community of individuals who can and do affect the world for the better. *Big Vision* might also help foster understanding about the nature and experience of us small-business owners for family members, friends, and employees—those closest to us and most affected by the enterprise and its demands on us.

How to Use This Book

I've organized *Big Vision, Small Business* with small-business owners in mind. You can read the book cover to cover, if you're so moved, or you can start with the "Key" that speaks to you most and begin your reading in that section. Either way, the book is designed to serve as a resource you can keep at arm's length for those days when you need an idea, a new perspective, or a little inspiration.

The book is intended to validate, challenge, and expand readers' current knowledge and experience base. In that spirit, I've included chapters that are more conceptual and data oriented and provide a bird's-eye view of small enterprise and its contributions and strengths. Other chapters provide personal anecdotes and insights from my own journey, as well as those of the 70-plus business owners I interviewed. In addition, I've suggested reflection points and questions that you can jot in your notebook for personal reflection or dialogue with others in your group. I haven't dumbed the content down, since I know that readers are smart enough to head for their dictionary or other reference if there's a new term or concept within these pages.

Here's what follows:

Section One, *There's More Than One Way to Define Growth,* introduces the concept of qualitative, rather than quantitative, growth. Since you can't leverage small-enterprise attributes if you don't know what they are, it offers a key to what small business is and what contributions small enterprises make to their local communities and the larger economy. It begins to point out the perspectives and practices that distinguish a big-vision small business from the larger category of small business. This section also reviews the advantages and disadvantages of large- versus small-scale enterprise, introduces a way to look at growth as a qualitative issue rather than a solely quantitative one, and shares in-depth profiles of four big-vision small-business owners and their "growth rich" journeys. It also clarifies the importance of making conscious decisions about growth and sets the stage for the next three keys to success, which offer pathways to qualitative growth while helping to strengthen what are traditionally considered small-business advantages.

Section Two, *To Live Large, You Have to Vision Big,* brings to life the saying "If you don't know where you're going, any road will do." Big-vision small-business owners create a clear vision of their reason for being in business, and that vision sustains them through flush and tough times alike. This section includes the 12 priorities of big-vision small businesses; reviews definitions of vision, mission, and values as they relate to a big-vision small enterprise; and emphasizes the importance of having a plan to help integrate your vision with the everyday actions of the business. You'll also find an in-depth profile that shows how one big-vision small-business owner relied on clear vision and daily perseverance while navigating intense challenges as she created her enterprise. As with the first section, there are thought-provoking and insight-generating questions, reflection points, and exercises included in the content.

Section Three, *Right Relationship Is a Big-Vision Craft,* looks deeply into an area where big-vision small businesses can reign supreme: personalized, thoughtful relationships. More than just a surface-skimming view of customer service or a review of how to find "human capital" or win the "war for talent," this section discusses why and how a big-vision enterprise owner can take communication and relationship building to a higher level, where right relationship is both a distinguishing factor, a means of qualitative growth, and even an avenue for deepening wisdom and personal mastery. Stemming from the Buddhist Eightfold Path, and inspired by other spiritual traditions as well, right relationship challenges us to a higher standard of mindfulness and excellence in our connections with others. While the section focuses on relationships with employees and customers, the tenets can and should be expanded outward to include all stakeholders affected by the organization. Since right relationship is a hands-on discipline, this section offers many tips for practical application from big-vision small-enterprise leaders, as well as high-level concepts and ideals.

Section Four, *To Live from the Source, Replenish the Well,* explores the ways that what I call wisdom and mastery practices provide inspirational fuel to help guide and sustain a big-vision, small-business owner in running such an enterprise. It includes chapters on wisdom and spirituality in the workplace and delves into several of the common challenge areas that both require and develop wisdom and mastery: money and risk, competition, success and failure, and time management. There is also a chapter of essays or reflections on various practices that a business owner might adopt to foster such concepts.

Finally, the book closes with a few thoughts and suggestions to help you begin to engage more fully with the ideas shared throughout the book.

The anecdotes, stories, lessons, and suggestions contained within these pages come from a variety of sources: my own decade of experience as a business owner, countless informal conversations with business owners over the years, and more formal interviews with small-business owners and advocates from throughout the United States. For the interviews, I contacted small-business organizations, such as Chambers of Commerce and Small Business Development Centers, and asked for referrals to those individuals in their communities who fit the profile of a big-vision small-business owner. I spoke with business owners or organization representatives from nearly every region of the United States and corresponded with colleagues throughout the world.

At the same time, I continued my informal discussions and routine patronage of small businesses in my own neighborhood and city and in areas I've visited during the course of writing this book. The most wonderful thing is how similar most of the people I spoke with found the experience of business ownership and how inspiring it was to talk to a group of people so committed to, in some way, being of service and enriching the lives or experiences of others through the operation of their small businesses.

This book isn't intended to be The Answer. It's not designed to be The Small-Business Gospel, nor a lofty academic tome. It isn't a template for tax preparation or outlining a business plan, since there is plenty of information already available on those topics. While providing ideas, insights, and food for both thought and application, this book is not a replacement for seeking tailored counsel from your attorney, certified public accountant, spiritual counselor, or others from whom you seek guidance on issues specific to you and your business. And none of these are substitutes for your own reflection, intuition, and experience about what's right for your business as it relates to you, your family, your life, and your mission or purpose in the world.

My greatest hope is that *Big Vision, Small Business* serves as an inspiration to help you, at various junctures in your small-business journey, to assess the options, make a decision that's right for you at that point, and perhaps, adopt a mindset that allows the journey to be fulfilling and energizing rather than draining. I hope it helps you, in these challenging times, find greater meaning and create deepened connections. May you find comfort, insight, and enthusiasm from the wisdom shared by actual small-business owners who have stood at the doorway of possibility opened by a vision only they could see, and have faced and surmounted again and again the day-to-day challenges inherent in manifesting that vision. My hat is off to you for having the courage to undertake the journey, and even more for deciding to make your enterprise extraordinary instead of mediocre. Your community and the world are better for it!

Jamie Walters
San Francisco, 2002

Acknowledgments

WRITING A BOOK is a lot like creating a business. Both are more marathons than they are sprints, and both are intensely rewarding and soul-expanding endeavors. And while both seem like solitary efforts, they are often completed thanks to the participation and support of others.

I'm grateful to many people, not the least of whom are my fellow business owners, who, in a spirit of trust and generosity, shared their experiences and insights with me in a host of formal interviews and less formal conversations. I'm also grateful to the many big-vision small-enterprise owners and spiritual leaders whose work and dedication has inspired me along the way. Their wisdom personalizes and enriches these pages, to the benefit of others who will read this book. Many of the people with whom I spoke are not featured specifically by name or company, though the spirit of each is present in the contents of this book.

I've enjoyed working with the dedicated team at Berrett-Koehler—itself a big-vision small business. I particularly appreciate fellow B-K author David Korten's referral and Steven Piersanti's very keen and insightful questions, which challenged me to sharpen my focus and better develop the book's core strengths. To all of the B-K team: it's a genuine pleasure to work with you.

Thanks to Sarah Fenson, my Ivy Sea, Inc., colleague, whose reliability helped me create the time to write both editions of this book; to Karla Toland, who, in addition to reading the manuscript, created the incredible resin piece for the cover art; to Misha Bruk for photographing the cover art; to Shelby Putnam Tupper for designing the jacket; to Claude Whitmyer, Judith Kautz, and Terri Lonier for their time and thought in reviewing the original manuscript; and to Lawrence Ellis, Lylie Fisher, Adam Leonard, Kathleen Epperson, Sara Jane Hope, Jean Ortega, and Jeffrey Kulick for providing thoughtful suggestions for improving the manuscript for the paperback edition.

Special thanks to my sister, Teri Walters, for lending her keen eye in the editing and proof stages; and to my sister Mandi Walters for her encouragement. To my mom and dad: it's always fortifying to know that you're proud of me no matter what I do, so long as I keep my integrity, strive to be decent and kind to others, and follow my vision of what's possible. And to my ancestors who watch over me, I feel your strength and presence every day.

Thanks, too, to Jo Madrid and Marie Seger, from whom I get invaluable guidance in managing my energy and mindset, minding my intuition, and staying on my spiritual as well as my business path. There are many other people to whom I am grateful for their example or advice along the way. Though I can't name them all here, I send them thanks and blessings in my prayers.

Last, but certainly not least, much appreciation goes to my husband and business partner, Tom Tshontikidis, for reminding me to be patient, talking through my ideas for the book, providing never ending support and encouragement, reading through drafts, and working side-by-side with me as we got our "real world" experience that informs each section of the book. Tom, it's always fun.

KEY № 1:
THERE'S MORE
THAN ONE WAY TO
DEFINE GROWTH

"Decide what you want,

decide what you are

willing to exchange for it.

Establish your priorities

and go to work."

H. L. Hunt

"There are many ways of

going forward, but only

one way of standing still."

Franklin D. Roosevelt

OUR OBSESSION WITH SIZE creates a number of challenges for the owner of a small business: perceptual challenges regarding the relationship between size and success, for example, as well as the assumption that a business must grow quantitatively or die, a business commandment *Inc. Magazine* featured as a New Economy Myth.[1] For the steward of a big-vision small business, the conflict between an internally motivated desire to build a distinguished organization and the externally motivated desire to create a company that is successful according to cultural norms can be significant, even paralyzing; it is the golden carrot that can lure us down the wrong path, where we may well find that the sparkling gold was merely a thin, colored-foil wrapper.

So how might we know the difference between the real golden carrot and the foil-covered one? This awareness—between the genuine and the superficial, the qualitative and the quantitative—is one factor that sets the big-vision small-business owner apart from her or his small-business peers. This section will begin to explore the distinctions between small and large enterprises and between qualitative and quantitative growth, and how all of these issues play out in the day-to-day lives of big-vision, small-business owners.

Chapter 1

FINDING QUALITY IN
THE LAND OF QUANTITY

FINDING EVIDENCE of quantity worship isn't difficult, even in the midst of so-called small-business advocates. Take, for example, Small Business Week, an event sponsored in May 2000 by the U.S. Small Business Administration (SBA). After referencing some of the contributions made by small businesses to our economy, the organization's Web site went on to list the selection criteria for Small Business Person of the Year, emphasizing growth in the number of employees and increase in sales or unit volume as indicators of success. The SBA also has defined as "small" those businesses with up to 500 employees, a size most owners of truly small businesses consider very comfortably midsized, or even large.[2]

In a smaller but no less insidious example, one of the business owners interviewed for this book was named employer of the year by a statewide professional association in recognition of his employee relations practices. In the press release announcing the honor, the association representative referred to the award-winning business as "a small *but* growing firm," as if the small group that warranted such recognition in the first place wasn't quite enough. Seemingly trivial, perhaps, but language matters because it reflects deeply held assumptions and perpetuates an inappropriately narrow view of small business. These examples are just two indications of our culture's unhealthy and often thoughtless bias toward big.

Surely increased sales or employee count provides one definition of growth but not the only one, and not one that guarantees profitability or success, much less a positive impact on the community or good quality of life for its founders. After all, one has to look no further than the recently worshipped, fast-growth dot-com companies to know that rapid expansion, in terms of employees and capital commitment, doesn't guarantee a solid business concept, sustainability, profitability, nor economic (not to mention qualitative) contribution.

But just as expanded size doesn't equate with profitability, satisfaction, or success, neither does an advocacy for refined smaller enterprises eschew the need for profitability and good business judgment. Personally, my advocacy for what author and economist David Korten has called the human-scale, locally accountable enterprise is inseparable from my preference for a good standard of living, which includes a self-defined degree of financial freedom. A preference for small business is not, for me, synonymous with a vow of poverty. It is, however, inseparable from knowing what is enough and what is—at the end of the day or of one's life—truly important.

So if we're willing to step away from our torrid cultural affair with size and linear progressions even for a moment, we might allow that growth can also mean an evolution or transformation, with an emphasis on qualitative aspects of business ownership, personal development, and contribution to the community. Unlike the more traditional, numerically focused entrepreneurs, big-vision small-business owners define growth in just this way—more a matter of polishing a gem and perfecting its facets, if you will, than of acquiring an ever expanding number of gems regardless of quality or of the fact that they might be permanently depleting the mine. Ultimately, the choice regarding what's most appropriate must be left to the business owner, whose business, family, and life are most affected by this very personal decision.

The problem is that the decision to grow quantitatively is rarely driven by a reflection on one's personal preferences or an assessment of other ways the organization might continue to live and thrive. Too often, the decision to expand is a result of an unquestioning acceptance of the "grow or die" myth, when in fact the end product of this approach might well be "grow *and* die."

What are you the small-business owner to do in the face of such questions? Consider that there might be more than one way to grow, reflect on your options, decide what path is most consistent with your vision for your quality of life and desired contribution to the world, and then determine how business size or evolution can provide the best vehicle.

Chapter 2

APPRECIATING THE POWER
OF SMALL ENTERPRISE

WE LIVE IN A CULTURE that engages in what E. F. Schumacher, in his book *Small Is Beautiful,* referred to as the "idolatry of large size." Despite this, many enterprise owners still opt to keep their organizations small in size and big in vision and craftsmanship. Others, however, succumb to the myth that adding locations, employees, and revenues is the only route to growth and success, even if such a course conflicts with other lifestyle goals or the founding vision of the enterprise. Many even pursue quantitative growth, though it ultimately results not just in the erosion of their vision but in the failure of their company as well. Why? And what choices exist to help make growth-related decisions more deliberate and thoughtful?

One problem is rooted, again, in our assumptions. We assume that, because politicians talk about "helping small business" and large corporations create advertisements extolling the virtues of small business, we have a culture in which people actually demonstrate appreciation for the challenges and contributions of individual small enterprises. We too easily mistake the talk about small business being the engine of the economy, or the buzz about how the smallest businesses consistently create more jobs than their colossal brethren, or that woman-owned companies alone employ more people than the Fortune 500, or the enormous richness of the small-business market, for actual appreciation of small business.

The reality is that small businesses—and I'm not talking about the proliferation (and even more recent demise) of many dot-com Internet startup companies—make an enormous contribution to our neighborhoods, our cities, and our nations. Collectively, the smallest businesses form a force to be recognized and reckoned with. Individually, small businesses offer ideas, innovations, practices, and lifestyle options that larger companies increasingly and unsuccessfully attempt to imitate. But small businesses are what they are and contribute what they contribute because of their size. Similarly, many little, low-budget independent movies that have generated a big grassroots following in the past decade have taken the film industry by storm because they are *not* products of the large corporate studios. The larger studios can more easily create blockbuster epics and marketing juggernauts, while the greater degree of originality and creativity—both in the art of film and grassroots marketing—more often comes from the budget-challenged independents.

"Growth for the sake of growth is the ideology of the cancer cell."

EDWARD ABBEY

The issue is not so much that large corporations are overappreciated but rather that the smallest enterprises are underestimated and underappreciated. Given that small organizations make such a significant contribution to the economy and the communities in which they're located and provide a wonderful vehicle for creating a good quality of life and being of service, the problem is that so few people fully understand and appreciate these very real contributions. To a degree, rhetoric is mistaken for action. The bottom line is that we have work to do in raising the awareness of the true merits of small-size big-impact enterprises. Big-vision small-business owners—whether by example or overt advocacy—promote the virtues and possibilities of a vision- and integrity-driven small enterprise.

A true appreciation will mean that the organizations that lobby on behalf of small enterprise must focus on the vast majority of their constituency—the smallest enterprises, not the larger-scale operations. Heightened awareness will mean that their lobbying should result in policies that better support the small office/home office (SOHO) demographic of enterprises that have fewer than 20 people. It will also mean that local officials won't blindly welcome big-box retailers into the community without simultaneously creating plans to ensure a robust small-business community and that small-business owners won't let their assumptions regarding growth dictate their decisions and the quality of both business and life.

What Is a Small Business?

Before looking at some of the contributions small enterprises make, you may be asking, "What exactly constitutes a small business?" It's a good question and a necessary one if we're to discern the general contributions of small business or discuss the unique merits of big-vision small business. Unfortunately, relying on current data or definitions yields more than one answer.

We've seen that U.S. agencies such as the Small Business Administration often categorize a small business as any enterprise with 500 or fewer employees, though in other cases they define a small business as having fewer than 100 employees and a microenterprise as having 19 or fewer people. Chambers of Commerce report that the majority of their members—70 to 90 percent—are enterprises with 20 or fewer, which is the range used by Working Solo, Inc., a SOHO-market consulting firm, to define a SOHO enterprise.[3] In the United Kingdom, most small-business advocates use a standard of up to nine people for a microenterprise, 49 or fewer for small business, 50 to 249 employees for a medium-size firm, and 250-plus for a large company. The European Union defines microenterprises as having fewer than 10 employees, small businesses as those with up to 50.[4] Other organizations use a variety of measures, recognizing that industry plays some role in defining what a small business is, since "small" in manufacturing might be 50 while that number might constitute a large enterprise if applied to a florist, printer, or typical consultancy.

While the lack of common, contemporary definitions for *small business* is troublesome, perhaps worse still is the fact that, according to the U.S. Census Bureau, the single-person enterprises that make up close to 75 percent of all U.S. businesses aren't even included in many statistical surveys.[5] Why? Because most have lower overhead and no one but the owner on payroll and thus comprise only 3 percent of business tax receipts. So despite their sheer number and despite their overall economic and cultural importance, this group of SOHOs is invisible to the government, at least for the purposes of having access to business-supportive policies and resources that stem from statistical prominence.

The multitude of definitions of *small business* and the exclusion of most self-employed or single-person enterprises from many statistical surveys and reports create problems in discussing and meeting the needs of the majority of small-business owners. The U.S. government hasn't yet caught up to the reality of solo or SOHO entrepreneurship. According to the SBA Office of Advocacy's 1998 State of Small Business report to the president, "static data cannot be used to measure dynamic change."[6] While SOHOs are increasingly recognized for their economic and cultural importance in other countries, SOHO-supportive policy making consistently lags in all countries, particularly the United States. Yet even while imperfect, the existing data can be pieced together and mined for clues as to why small business—and particularly big-vision small business—is so vitally important from both economic and cultural perspectives.

I've elected to rely upon the SBA microenterprise or SOHO definition of 20 or fewer people, since many of the big-vision business tenets can be more deeply explored and adopted in groups of this size or smaller, for reasons I share throughout this book. Since most statisticians rely on a variety of numerical definitions for small business or are altogether vague about what measure they're using, it's not always possible to include breakdowns of statistics as they relate specifically to SOHOs.

The Contributions of Small Business to Society

The good news is that the value and increasing visibility of microenterprises and SOHOs is resulting in additional research to quantify the contributions made by this particular group of enterprises. Even people who readily quip, "Small businesses are the engine of the economy," are often very surprised when presented with the specific reasons that underscore the truth of this statement, including the fact that the majority of those small businesses are, indeed, very small in size. Do you have doubts about the clout of the smallest companies, particularly those that are both aware of and intent upon leveraging these potential strengths? Consider the following:[7]

THE SMALLEST BUSINESSES ARE NUMEROUS

Nearly three-quarters of all U.S. businesses are self-employed individuals with no one else on payroll and are responsible for $580 billion in sales. SOHOs, those small enterprises with 20 or fewer employees, comprise one of the fastest-growing market segments, with more than 31 million SOHO enterprises in the United States as of 2001, spending an average of $103 billion each year. According to the Entrepreneurial Research Consortium, another 7 million people are considering business ownership or self-employment. All of these sectors—self-employed persons, home-based offices, small offices—are expected to grow in number and strength in the coming years. These statistics make clear that the vast majority of businesses are not just small businesses but very small businesses, and they're an increasingly relevant group economically and culturally.

THE SMALLEST BUSINESSES CREATE JOBS

In fact, small enterprises don't just create a few jobs, they create the majority of jobs, representing 99.7 percent of all employers in the United States. Between 1992 and 1998, small U.S. firms created nearly all of the 12 million net new jobs. The smallest of those, businesses with fewer than 20 employees, generated more than two-thirds of the new jobs. Firms with fewer than five employees generated just over half of those new jobs. The Office of Advocacy also reports that small enterprises are more likely to employ inexperienced and older workers; offer greater opportunities for women, minorities, and immigrants; and provide welfare-to-work or other opportunities for financial self-sufficiency. Since home-based and small-office businesses are both numerous and resilient, they create jobs directly through their own hiring, and also their spending. After all, SOHOs purchase office furniture, supplies, telephones, computers, bank services, and all of the other products and services necessary to run a business—products that often come from larger companies and whose purchase stimulates the creation of jobs to support manufacturing, shipping, and sales.

The Smallest Businesses
Foster Economic Diversity

Small businesses help create a more diverse, resilient economy, allowing a greater variety of products, industries, and participants. Unlike one-company or single-industry towns, communities with a healthy contingent of small, locally owned enterprises are less vulnerable to a recession or an economic downturn that affects a particular industry. In this way, economic diversity fosters a greater degree of local self-reliance than would be the case when a locality relies too heavily on a small number of large corporations whose fortunes are tied to the fickleness of Wall Street analysts or global market shifts and whose investors and decision makers may live far from (and thus care little about) that community. And as the Office of Advocacy's State of Small Business report emphasized, the smallest enterprises contribute to diversity through innovation and creativity and offer opportunity for both self-sufficiency in financially disadvantaged communities and advancement for minorities, women, and immigrants.

The Smallest Businesses
Contribute Uniqueness

In addition to featuring an environment defined by the personality of an individual business owner, small enterprises offer a more unique array of merchandise and a more personalized buyer-seller connection or service level that augments the products and services offered by large corporations or chain stores. If you visited five cities that had only chain stores, the stores of each chain would differ little from one another, but you'd know what to expect regarding the atmosphere, merchandise, and service. When you add local boutiques, bakeries, restaurants, and bookstores to the mix, the places take on a more unique flavor that makes each more of an adventure for the visitor, and more like home for those who live there.

The Smallest Businesses
Offer Quality of Life

Small enterprises are personal enterprises, often focusing on the community or region and increasingly operating wholly or at least occasionally from a home-based office. A small-business owner has more control over decision making that affects the time he spends with his family or on other non-business interests, as well as over decisions that affect the quality of his own workday. If there is a schedule conflict, he can more easily choose to plan around it. If an ideal project or client profile crops up, she can choose to plant the seeds that will grow those opportunities in her business garden for the next season.

In addition, small businesses are often associated with community service and the quality of life of others. Examples of small business–dominated service industries include restaurants, retail services, outpatient care facilities, health care–provider offices, residential care facilities, special trade construction contractors, architectural and engineering services, computer and data-processing services, day care providers, job training, and counseling and rehabilitation services. Such industries accounted for about 64 percent of the 2.5 million new jobs created in 1996 alone. And that's not the extent of small businesses' contributions to local quality of life. Small businesses donate more in cash and in-kind services—$800 per employee—than do their large-organization counterparts.[8]

DAVID AND GOLIATH

This isn't to say that big companies or even megacorporations are irrelevant or unnecessary. They have their place and the potential to make a positive contribution as well, particularly in areas requiring large-scale manufacturing, mass distribution. Even a company like Apple Computer, whose sales account for less than 5 percent of the computer market,[9] requires a sizeable employee base to conceptualize, design, manufacture, and distribute its products in their competitive industry. The same could be said for larger companies that manufacture and distribute lifesaving medical equipment and medications, for example, and transportation and communications companies that help connect those in need with the people and products that can improve health, community, and quality of life. These examples demonstrate areas where a larger organization *can* be more effective than an informal network of small enterprises.

Proponents of large corporations also note, justifiably, that these companies also create jobs and provide employment and a sense of community for people who prefer being a part of a larger enterprise. While it is a myth that large firms create the majority of jobs or provide more-secure employment, given the regularity with which they swell their ranks only to lay employees off in droves, large corporations often have the greater financial resources necessary for such things as employer-matched retirement programs, subsidized health plans, on-site day care or cafeterias for workers, and funding for social-responsibility initiatives. These are benefits many employees find desirable in their search for some degree of perceived security. Yet not everyone agrees that such benefits ensure security, much less provide an indication of actual caring for the employee or other stakeholders.

This was evidenced by the collapse and ensuing ethical scandal involving Enron Corporation in 2002, where the crack in the company's "good corporate citizen" veneer revealed a plethora of unethical practices and organizational culture norms that resulted in significant loss and pain for both employees and average investors. Big-vision small-business owners, while perhaps not having the economies of scale to offer such lucrative financial perks as Enron had, would not choose such unethical and deceptive practices. Nor would their small size and local visibility allow them to conceal such practices easily (or make them as immune to accountability afterwards).

> "Never doubt that a small group of thoughtful, committed people can change the world. Indeed, it is the only thing that ever has."
>
> MARGARET MEAD

According to author, professor, and sustainable-business advocate David Korten, the corporation is a legal instrument created for the purposes of making money, rather than an entity concerned with community stewardship or quality of life. In a dialogue with Paul Hawken in *Yes! A Journal of Positive Futures,* Korten emphasizes that the greater contribution is made by more mindful, human-scale enterprises—such as local bakeries, small farms, boutiques, hardware and book stores, and cafes—whose owners live and work in the community and are therefore accountable for their effect on the local quality of life.[10] While a large enterprise might itself provide an on-site day care, gym, dry cleaner, or cafeteria, for instance, a network of small businesses within a community can offer the same.

When considering the value contributed by large versus small organizations, one isn't necessarily better than the other, but one or the other may be a better career and lifestyle choice, and organizational size does affect the organization's ability to remain true to its vision. Such consideration most definitely challenges commonly held assumptions regarding both large and small business. Regardless, the smallest businesses—those place-based, human-scale organizations Mr. Korten describes—are able to make a significant positive contribution to sustaining the healthier workplaces and communities where most of us spend a good deal of time.

So small businesses contribute in both tangible and intangible ways to the communities in which they reside, a point reinforced by the renaissance in downtown revitalization and the trend toward new downtown centers under development in so-called soulless suburbia. According to journalist Craig Savoye of the *Christian Science Monitor,* 30 to 40 new downtowns are planned or completed in suburban communities, and about 6,000 cities have downtown renovations in progress. Why? According to Savoye and others, people have an increasing need for local community as the world becomes faster, more global, and technology-driven. Savoye dubs the trend "a civil war against the United States of Generica."[11] What's the typical vision of the quintessential downtown? Rows of Main Street–style small businesses offering personalized service, a sense of community, and a variety of nonhomogeneous shopping options and providing an array of high-quality services that also support the needs of an area's larger corporations. In our "post-9/11" world, a higher degree of personalization, humanity, and connection—not to mention local self-reliance to help protect a bit against global shockwaves—become more important than ever.

Vision-inspired businesses aim to consciously make qualitative contributions, and these average-yet-extraordinary people invest their time, passion, energy, money, and other resources to create and sustain such businesses. The following chapters take a look at some pros and cons of operating a small versus large business and share real-world stories of how four big-vision small-business owners came face to face with choices regarding qualitative and quantitative growth.

Chapter 3

WHICH IS BETTER, BIG OR SMALL?

FOR A MORE DELIBERATE consideration of what growth can and should mean for an individual business and its owner, you might begin with an understanding of the advantages and disadvantages of small versus large organizations. This seems an obvious point, but it's amazing how frequently business owners overlook this consideration in the face of external pressure to add people, revenues, production capacities, or locations. In truth, opting to have fewer employees or one location is the perfect choice for some small-business owners, while growing in size is a necessity for others. Big-vision small-business owners make sure they're not just aware of but building upon the strengths associated with small-size enterprise, just as they know about and work around the disadvantages. Indeed, they view this very exercise as an opportunity for qualitative growth. So what makes them decide to revel in small size? And at what cost and benefit?

THE PROS AND CONS OF SMALL SIZE

The advantages of small-scale organizations or groups are matters of quality and depth—of vision, relationships, communication, adaptability, evolution, creativity, and contribution. And quality of life. Qualitative excellence—that master-craftsman level of refinement—goes to the very heart of what's more possible in a small group.

According to group dynamics experts, the optimal size for a highly functioning group is five people.[12] Why just five? In a group this size, there are enough participants to allow for multiple perspectives but few enough to avoid the separation into divisive factions that begin to hinder efficiency and the quality of relationships in larger groups. Also, the smaller the group, the greater the opportunity for personalized connection (and the personal accountability that such visibility demands) and the less need there is for bureaucratic processes, systems, and layers. These are some of the reasons that Navy SEAL teams and other highly specialized units tend to have eight or fewer people.

What are some of the specific qualitative factors that distinguish an effective small group, the kind that big-vision small-business owners consciously cultivate and put to work?

· SMALL GROUPS CAN BE MORE EFFICIENT.

Without layers of corporate hierarchy (which are required to run a larger organization effectively), the small enterprise is less bureaucratic and more nimble. Its response time is quicker because the distance between "decide" and "do" is much shorter. Just by virtue of their size, small enterprises require less overhead—office space, supplies, payroll, equipment, furniture, insurance—which can translate into lower expenses and, in some cases, lower fees.

· SMALL GROUPS CAN BE MORE CREATIVE.

Innovation is a hallmark of smaller enterprises, again in part due to the lack of hierarchy and bureaucracy that hampers the chaos required for creativity. Innovation applies not only to product development, though about 50 percent of new inventions are associated with small firms, but also to creative approaches to providing services. A large organization finds its efficiency and reliability in order, quality control, process, and the hierarchy necessary to keep the many units of a large enterprise functioning compatibly.

· SMALL GROUPS CAN BE MORE PERSONAL.

For the same reasons, a small enterprise can offer a more personalized connection to the customer or delivery of a product or service.

Because it has fewer people and locations, and presumably lower overhead expenses, a small enterprise is able to offer deeper connections and be more selective in its work. The vision can be more connected to personal interests, spiritual beliefs, and lifestyle preferences. Communication can be more personal, less formal or systematized. The greater the overhead and distribution and the more complex the organization, the more the focus turns to quantifiable processes, activities, and measures that generate the revenue needed to sustain the enterprise and provide profit to a broader array of shareholders. As it grows in size and overhead and becomes more dependent on external investors, the organization moves by necessity from a subjective, personal focus on building relationships to a more objective, process focus on generating revenues.

· SMALL GROUPS CAN BE MORE SPECIALIZED.

As is the case with right relationships, which is a form of specialization, a small enterprise can distinguish itself by offering depth rather than breadth, a greater level of distinctiveness and craftsmanship instead of the quantity a large-scale operation can provide. Whereas a larger organization or multilocation franchise relies upon standard processes and tolerates fewer deviations in order to meet operating goals, a small enterprise can personalize, customize, experiment, and even be downright quirky in its product offerings and service delivery.

· SMALL GROUPS CAN BE MORE FLEXIBLE.

Just as small boats can turn more quickly than large ocean liners, small enterprises can shift and adapt more quickly than can large corporations. Why? Several factors lend themselves to flexibility: fewer layers, lower overhead, and greater compactness or localization. Greater flexibility can translate into benefits such as an ability to accommodate customer preferences or requests and responsiveness to abrupt market shifts. Small size and independent ownership more easily translate into a greater willingness to take risks or deviate from the business plan, which is less likely in a publicly owned corporation that is expected to deliver ever increasing profits to investors. This may be one reason that market niches can be more readily exploited by smaller, innovative firms, with some of the resulting products and services adopted and expanded by large corporations with greater resources and reach.

· SMALL GROUPS CAN BE MORE ACCOUNTABLE.

As is the case in any tight-knit community, breaches of trust and responsibility are more immediately visible and have a more immediate effect. In a small group, for better or worse, there is literally no place to escape accountability. Individuals in a small enterprise can't hide behind a huge brand or public-relations machine nor lurk unnoticed in one of hundreds of cubicles in corporate campus buildings. If someone doesn't do his job, it doesn't get done, and everyone knows it. The visibility and small margin for error in a small business create a more stringent requirement for personal efficiency and accountability. In a large enterprise, timelines stretch, and committees, departments, or operating divisions, not individuals, become the focus for organizational performance-related expectations. If one branch of a well-established company—a large advertising agency, for example—botches a project or loses a client, it doesn't affect the other units unless the backlash is enormous. A large enterprise absorbs such occurrences more easily. A small group is more immediately and significantly affected.

· SMALL GROUPS CAN BE MORE RESILIENT.

The owners and principal members of a small enterprise are so personally invested in the business that failure is not an option. The small organization is more about the idea, the vision, which continues to exist regardless of market cycles, infrastructure shifts, or even individual failures. Small enterprises can also be more resilient because of the familylike dynamic and thus the personal connection with or investment in the organization's vision and survival.[13] Closing one's business or leaving one's enterprise is like divorcing one's own identity or family; it happens, but is less likely to occur without a deeper level of thoughtfulness, particularly in a big-vision small business that has cultivated the vision, fostered the level of relationship, and enhanced the meaningfulness of the work by connecting personal interests—or even a vocational calling—to organizational mission.

Reflection Point

· How would you evaluate your group against the above strengths?

· How does your group leverage these strengths?

· Are there strengths that you associate with your enterprise that aren't on this list?

Disadvantages of Small-Scale Enterprise

And what of the limitations or disadvantages of being purposefully small-scale? As with everything, choosing to keep an enterprise small in size has a shadow side. Whether the shadow factors are a problem or a catalyst to creativity is a matter of choice and circumstance. The very strengths of small enterprise can turn on their heads to become limitations. For example, the primary disadvantages associated with small enterprises or groups include:

· Limits in distribution capacity

· Limits in access to funding

· Limits in breadth of services or products

· Limits in objectivity

These areas are often identified as large-company advantages, and with good reason. Manufacturing and distributing a product requires more people, equipment, and supplies. If you need a reliable network for coast-to-coast or worldwide transportation, it may be somewhat chaotic to count on a large number of two-person enterprises. While not immune to its own challenges, a large corporate structure can provide the consistency and stability required for endeavors that are geographically far-reaching. Having more people, equipment, and supplies requires greater access to capital, and a tangible inventory also increases the likelihood of obtaining the necessary financing, even if the corporation is troubled. This was evidenced with Kmart's bankruptcy in 2002, when the company received access to $2 billion in loans even though its performance record had been poor and its future viability was sharply questioned. In addition, the checks and balances of multiple levels of hierarchy, and the need to report to outside investors, can increase the need for objectivity in researching, planning, and moving ahead with new initiatives.

As an enterprise moves from qualitative to quantitative business, or from services to material products, it becomes more focused on objective, quantifiable, external factors and less reliant on deeply personal vision, preferences, intuition, inspiration, or relationships. That the former can be more readily quantified puts bankers at ease, and makes it easier to associate the enterprise's function with the standard activities of the industrial age. Enterprises that rely more on personality, relationship, and service are harder to quantify, more difficult for data-focused people to understand. And thus they seem riskier than do the quantifiable, tangible enterprises. Though the massive dot-com failures and other corporate ethics scandals demonstrate the shortcomings of this thinking, it is nonetheless the norm in policy and finance circles, which might otherwise, with greater awareness, be more supportive of small-scale enterprise.

What's more, being a member of a small, SOHO-size business, with its deeply personal connections and high levels of personal visibility, can be too painful for some people. This is particularly true when the leader and employees of the enterprise wallow in familial dysfunction and don't practice the tenets of a big-vision small business.

And how do these themes play out with real-world organizations? According to Keith Rollins of The Resource Hub, the one-stop entrepreneurial resource center in Portland, Maine, specialized consulting companies with a regional or local niche might choose to remain smaller in size, focusing attention and resources on honing skills in their area of experience and the service they deliver. A retailer who wishes to cultivate a unique inventory featuring local artisans might also do well to remain small in size and big in vision. If a company owner wishes to concentrate on a specific, exquisite-quality product, such as the uniquely illustrated leatherbound Bibles created by one successful San Francisco company, he might do well to cap quantitative growth to ensure that profitability doesn't require a product-line expansion or less exacting quality standards. Similarly, if a big-vision business owner wishes to maintain an unstructured or familial work environment in which right relationship is practiced with internal and external stakeholders, she might be better off limiting quantitative growth that would require a more formal, structured workplace.

Rollins agrees, however, that manufacturing businesses, for example, usually require a minimum number of people to produce their product and a larger number of people to expand the product line or the market reach. Oakland-based certified public accountant Sandy Collins, who advises many small-business owners, holds a similar perspective.

If you're in a retail environment or product-based business that is subject to standardized processes, then you can choose to grow in number more easily. Growth becomes more a function of finding the right people than of maintaining a highly specialized service or quality level. If you have processes, routines, and procedures documented, then anyone walking in with a minimum degree of skill or experience can do the job. But if what you focus on in your business is highly refined quality and personalized service, the smaller you stay the better you are, because you can hire for fit versus quantity, and continue to give your clients the high level of customized expertise and service they expect.

Collins also advises her clients to consider personal preferences, skills, and lifestyle goals in deciding whether to expand the business quantitatively:

If a business owner sees the business with the idea that they're going to sell it eventually, or they don't see themselves doing the same thing in 10 years, they might choose to grow a salable business. But other business owners have no interest in doing something different from their craft or the small niche market they've created. They don't want to do what happens to many unsuspecting business owners who choose to add people and expand facilities: they end up marketing, administrating operations, or managing people rather than doing what they started the business to do.

One thing is certain: a small-enterprise leader will be wise to consider and build upon the strengths associated with and more possible in a smaller group. A big-vision small-business owner, having reflected on (and for good reasons rejected) the lure of quantitative growth, turns to qualitative growth as a way of pursuing her vision, enhancing the business's competitive edge, deepening relationships, maintaining a particular lifestyle quality and balance, building wisdom or honing skills, and keeping the business fresh.

The next chapter takes a closer look at some of the assumptions concerning quantitative growth, helps to clarify the definition of qualitative growth, and is followed by a series of profiles of four big-vision small-business owners that help bring to life these growth-related issues and decisions.

Chapter 4

MOVING FROM QUANTITATIVE GROWTH
TO QUALITATIVE EVOLUTION

BIG-VISION SMALL-BUSINESS owners seek a definition of growth perhaps more aligned with evolution than quantitative expansion, focusing more on questions such as "How?" and "Why?" (versus "How big?"). Requirements for ongoing qualitative growth and mastery include having a clear, idealistic vision; a bridge between vision and action; an emphasis on creating right relationships; and a strong "supporting cast" of wisdom and mastery practices that both inspire and sustain.

But how do we begin to challenge our limited perception about the ways an organization can grow, much less challenge society by embracing a definition of growth or entrepreneurship that is outside the celebrated norm? We can start with a few prevailing definitions, strip them of common associations with size, and adapt them to meet the needs of a big-vision small-business owner—an entrepreneur who opts for deep refinement in the tradition of the master craftsman.

For example, in his 1999 *Leader to Leader* article, "The Growth Imperative," author and University of Michigan professor Noel Tichy emphasizes that leaders can find opportunities for growth in several areas: finding new ways to serve existing companies, finding new customers for existing products and services, or identifying new products or services for a new set of customers.[14] Though Tichy is talking mainly about large corporations that might routinely create new divisions to accommodate such growth, these categories are relevant to the big-vision small-business owner, who can plot out an evolutionary pathway to introduce these new ways of thinking and working.

Contributing another perspective on quantitative growth, Larry Greiner, in his classic 1972 *Harvard Business Review* article, "Evolution and Revolution as Organizations Grow," said that management, eager for quantitative growth, "overlooks critical development questions such as: Where has our organization been? Where is it now? And what do the answers to these questions mean for where we are going?" Instead of asking the necessary introspective questions, argued Greiner, organizational leaders are inclined to focus on external factors such as market performance, which are less relevant to an organization's guiding vision.[15] Small-business owners can certainly ask these very questions, among others, for a deeper understanding when they find themselves talking about numerical expansion.

Another assumption many business owners make is that growth is something that can be meticulously planned and managed. Not so, according to London Business School economist Paul Geroski. Based on Geroski's studies, growth in companies large and small is erratic and random, a pattern he calls a "random walk." In reviewing a variety of available data on company growth, Geroski challenged the popular notion that company growth can be analytically studied and predicted. In addition to the theory of random growth, Geroski found that growth is not so much affected by the general strength or weakness of the economy or the company's industry niche as it is by innovation.[16]

Unfortunately, these and other assumptions about growth lead some business owners right over the cliff. For instance, they may succumb to pressure applied by advisers and investors to expand the enterprise in order to survive and stay competitive. Such was the case of John Peterman, founder of the J. Peterman Company and proud owner of what is now a cautionary tale about the pitfalls of quantitative growth.

Peterman founded his retail company in 1987, after stumbling across a cowboy-style duster coat that he loved and thought others would as well. He was right. The J. Peterman Company, guided by Peterman's vision of retailing the romance of another era, became known for its creative inventory and readable catalog, which the company called its *Owner's Manual*. By the end of 1990, the company had grown quickly to more than 75 employees and nearly $20 million in revenues. The fast-growth path had also set the stage for the company's ultimate fall from grace into bankruptcy not 10 years later.

In hindsight, Peterman tracked the problem to the elements inherent in the rapid expansion, including hiring for numbers rather than fit; recruiting executives from outside the company while systems and processes were changing; shifting from the original vision and intuitive marketing style to a revenue-generating model preferred by financiers; and adopting other expansion-mode practices like more frequent direct mailings, the proliferation of J. Peterman retail stores, and a broadening of the inventory away from the company's original focus. Where the emphasis had once been on the romantic image, unique inventory, and creative style, it had been refocused on new ways to expand reach and grow revenues. The company collapsed under the pressure, and J. Peterman Company went into bankruptcy in 1999 and was purchased by Paul Harris Stores. The company's founder found himself without a company, and out of a job.[17]

In other cases, our choices regarding the size and evolution of our businesses are re-active—a result of unexpected and often unwelcome crises such as employee turnover, canceled projects or accounts, market fluctuations, or cash flow shortages. In the face of these types of common challenges, some business owners close shop or claim bankruptcy, while others dig deep to reconnect with their originating vision, find resolve, put together a turnaround plan, and begin a transformative journey that may require them to be more deliberate and aware regarding their expectations about—and options for—growth.

"But it's never a good idea to grow just because you're desperate, where you're hiring people who may not be right for your environment. It's better sometimes to call and reschedule clients so that when they do come in, they get the quality service that your reputation has been built on."

NINA UMMEL

Kevin Owens agrees, and offers a perspective about growth that has been hewn from personal experience. Owens cofounded Select Design, Ltd., in Burlington, Vermont, and quickly grew the enterprise from a two-person partnership to a company of 50 employees. His firm's growth spurt had its rewards but also created unforeseen problems that led Owens to new insights:

> It's a simple point, but easy to miss: We were so focused on capitalistic growth that we forgot ourselves and our families. It's a lot nicer feeling when we remind ourselves that we don't have to buy that new piece of equipment or hire 10 new people over the next year. We can, but we used to do that because we thought that's what everyone does, that's what a business is supposed to do. But that's not the way it has to be. The only reason to grow a business or make it different is if it makes our lives better, and if it affects us and our families positively.

Transformative Small-Business Journeys

Unfortunately, many business owners view organizational growth too narrowly, perceiving far fewer options than in fact exist. So it isn't until a crisis forces a decision that they review potential avenues for action. While we can certainly be creative in the face of crisis, if we wait until then our choices are often more limited. By looking at the experiences of other business owners regarding the journeys through which they and their companies have evolved, perhaps more of us will reflect on these options for growth before a crisis forces our hand or will choose more purposefully in the face of challenge.

What follows are honest profiles of the journeys taken by four big-vision small-business owners as their assumptions about business, growth, success, and meaning were challenged by recessions, booms, employee turnover, intellectual property theft, and a variety of other circumstances common in running a business. Each of these company owners has had frontline experience with quantitative growth and has found that the meaning of growth is far richer than they might have ever imagined. Their journeys became their teachers, and they share what they've learned. In reading the vignettes from these four big-vision enterprise leaders, you may recognize patterns and learn from their experiences, so that their stories can inform your own perceptions and decisions about growth as it relates to you and your business.

Chapter 5

PROFILES IN GROWTH

DID YOU EVER WISH you could step for a brief time from your world into someone else's small-business reality, just to gauge how others go about making crucial decisions, find out what they do when they make mistakes, or learn something you could use to refine your approach to your own business? Here's your chance. In this section, you'll meet four big-vision small-business owners—Stephen Marcus, Tony Canaletich, Shelby Putnam Tupper, and Nina Ummel. The profiles are snapshots into their experiences with and insights gained from growth that confronted or eluded them at some point on their journeys as business owners. Since each business owner's story is unique, the profiles vary in length and composition.

And yet there are similarities, too, in that the challenges they faced deepened their experience and knowledge base, demanded clarification of their vision and reasons for being in business, and altered their perspectives about growth. By sharing their stories, they help all big-vision small-business aspirants view their own enterprises and journeys with greater clarity, patience, inspiration, and wisdom.

Perseverance: The Journey of Stephen Marcus and AIRS International

No one knows the transformative power of unexpected challenges more than Stephen Marcus, founder and president of AIRS International, a San

Diego–based fragrance products company. After years in the fragrance industry, Marcus started his business in 1989 and appeared on the *Inc.* 500 list of fast-growth companies in 1993–94, having taken the company from $100,000 to $3 million in revenues in just a few years. It was in the mid-1990s, fresh off several high-growth years, that things started to unwind for Marcus and AIRS.

"You reach a point where you've got a place, you start buying equipment and hiring more people, and things are just rolling," says Marcus. "Then you decide you want to grow the company further, so you start hiring so-called professionals, and the people who helped you in your start-up phase start to seem antiquated in comparison."

For Marcus, hiring a series of senior people from outside the business was one key element that sent the company into a tailspin from which he spent several years recovering. In addition to Marcus's challenge with a growing staff that was increasingly in conflict, a glitch surfaced in the manufacturing process for a new product in which he'd made a significant investment. According to Marcus, the company consequently became vulnerable and fell prey to a less than ethical investor who, in short order, hired away several of his key staff members, along with the proprietary knowledge they possessed, and established a competing business. With the loss of knowledgeable employees and a subsequent lawsuit to prevent the new competitor from using its client lists and other confidential information, AIRS teetered on the brink of bankruptcy, and Marcus found himself at a crossroads. In the face of a severe financial and business crisis, Marcus said he opted to rise to the challenge, put together a plan, and go back to the basics of what made the company a success in its earlier years.

> *"The trouble with the rat race is when you win, you're still a rat."*
>
> LILY TOMLIN

"We've had a lot of expensive lessons about doing business," says Marcus, "but we've gotten through that period and out of the resulting debt." He adds that the things that made the company unique at the beginning, such as the inspired fragrances and the company's mythology-infused and story-rich packaging, ended up too easily in the hands of competitors. "But our competitors made the mistake of thinking that what they were copying was just packaging, and AIRS is about more than that," Marcus says of his vision of bringing people together in a greater appreciation of beauty and nature. According to Marcus, who now has the wisdom of hindsight, the experience wasn't without a silver lining, however stiff the challenges.

"In retrospect, it's clear that the crisis situation forced us to grow and get creative about what really distinguishes this company, and about who we really are," says Marcus, who went on to rebuild his team, redesign the product packaging, launch the company's Web site, and pursue new products and markets. While running the company isn't without fresh challenges, AIRS products can be found in a growing number of retail outlets, and Marcus feels the company is more grounded in its originating vision.

Redemption: The Journey of San Francisco Renaissance

For Tony Canaletich, cofounder and president of San Francisco Renaissance, expansion was the logical path during the real estate boom of the 1980s. His niche-concept renovation construction company grew to well over 100 employees, and he and his two business partners found themselves executives in a large, thriving business. More than a decade later, Canaletich is happily leading a smaller team of 14 employees in a transformed company that once again focuses on its originating vision and superior craftsmanship on some of San Francisco's oldest Victorian homes.

What happened to San Francisco Renaissance in the interceding decade? Nothing less than a total renovation of the business, a renewed appreciation for the advantages of a smaller, tightly managed organization, and an owner's reacquaintance with his founding vision for the company. "I started San Francisco Renaissance because I love these old houses in San Francisco and I hate seeing them torn down," Canaletich says. "So that mission of restoring Victorian houses, for me, has a very high value. I wanted to stick to the purity of my vision, which was either to build something that would last for at least a hundred years or to work on something that needed restoration in order to last another hundred years."

Like many business owners, Canaletich has the satisfaction and wisdom gained from persevering through a crisis that threatened the very existence of the business. A different feeling comes from being able to see and talk about such a challenge from the other side, having weathered the challenge a bit wiser and perhaps more resilient for his troubles, which started with the temptation to grow with an economic boom.

· EXPANSION

"It's tempting to grow, because your gross sales are easy to expand. The numbers go up, and it's exciting for everyone," Canaletich says. "New people come in and everyone sees the gold mine, but what they don't realize is that it's temporary. I've learned that market booms don't go on forever." Canaletich and his two partners rode the wave, increasing to 150 employees at the firm's numerical peak. And, as with many rapidly expanding companies, Canaletich saw what he now believes was a negative effect on the owners' roles, as well as on the quality of the firm's work, its organizational culture, and financial health. "We were doing so many jobs in the late 1970s that I didn't even know about half of them," he remembers. "We had supervisors, and I was basically an executive."

As the company grew in size and his role changed from craftsman to company officer, Canaletich found himself more distant from his clientele and field employees and more focused on getting increasing numbers of large accounts. As the client list grew, the company's mission—and stability—shifted. "We were going to be the biggest remodeling and reconstruction business in the Bay Area. That was our bottom-line goal," Canaletich says.

For many people in our culture, looking in from the outside, such a fast-growing business, with its 150 employees and hefty client list, appears the ultimate success. But not for Canaletich, who saw quality and financial issues—as well as the marked departure from his founding purpose—as increasing problems. First, the company's rapid growth required aggressive hiring. "When you're hiring for expansion, the pressure is so monumental to fill those slots and get the numbers up that you make compromises," he says regarding the fit between the employment candidates and the company's core vision. With the quickly growing roster of new employees and clients, quality deteriorated.

"We were in such expansion mode that our quality and customer service started to suffer," says Canaletich. "It's really hard, with new personnel and an old system, to keep that system running at 100-percent optimal. You find yourself maxed in terms of key personnel time and resources, and when the economy finally started to contract, we had clients out there who weren't as satisfied as they should have been; and those are the key clients you want when the business does slow down."

"Also, when there's a boom, you can borrow a lot of money to fund an expansion," says Canaletich. "We were able to get loans based on the amount of business we had at the time, and we were able to borrow more money than we'd be able to pay off, personally, if the business became no longer viable."

· CONTRACTION

When the construction industry flattened in the early 1980s, Canaletich and his partners found that their worst fear had come true. "We had all these construction loans out, but we were no longer doing several million dollars worth of business, and we were no longer able to pay the loans," he remembers. "We had to default on some of the loans but were lucky enough to be able to work with our bankers, who gave us time to pay back the money we owed."

The effects of the firm's financial crisis unfortunately didn't stop with renegotiating loan payment terms. Seeing that the company was on the brink of collapse, Canaletich decided to radically reorganize and return to the ideals upon which the business had been founded. A painful part of his reorganization plan was downsizing to 10 employees and having to go forward without the participation of his two business partners.

"It was a very devastating experience, and there was a great sense of shame," he offers candidly. "But I also thought, 'This could be an opportunity; this could be where I tailor this business to be more of a lifestyle than the expansion business it had become.' I realized that wasn't the lifestyle I wanted to live; it didn't make me feel good. What makes me feel good is doing a job well, knowing the client, making sure the job's done with a high standard of quality, and getting paid for it."

· REDEMPTION

Canaletich found himself wanting to rebuild the business not from the perspective of size but with a strong grounding in its vision and a connection to how craftspeople had once operated: "When the craft system was first developed, one's life and what one did for a living weren't separate, and certainly weren't separate from one's spiritual life."

With the gift of the wisdom gained from the crisis, Canaletich now caps expansion during building booms like the one San Francisco enjoyed during the 1990s, opting to add employees carefully to ensure a compatible devotion to high quality and the building craft. "If I allow myself no more than 25 percent expansion during a boom period, I can accommodate that with a minimal impact when the market contracts," he says. "I've learned to be realistic when business is booming, meaning I have a target for how many jobs I can do and what my gross sales are going to be, and I don't go beyond that. It's really learning to say 'no,' and knowing and sticking to the limits required by my business to function at its peak." And also learning, Canaletich says, not to succumb to the prevailing trends during a boom.

"It comes down to a choice you have to make, and not getting caught up in the mass hysteria," he says. "There's a momentum that seems to happen when the company is doing well and the economy is strong. It's like the Gold Rush, with a lot of speculation. The companies that emerge through that have a very clear vision of their capacities and their limits, and of what they want to achieve, and they stick to it regardless of the mass hallucination."

Renewal: The Journey of Shelby Designs & Illustrates

When the crisis at hand is the result of a blazing dot-com employment market and staff turnover, the stress and expense can be significant, and the whole experience can test the business owner's resolve. For Shelby Putnam Tupper,

founder of Shelby Designs & Illustrates in Oakland, California, a staffing crisis—during a period when demand for graphic designers was high and she was
starting a family—took her to near breakpoint and back to basics. The result? A
thorough spring cleaning and a renewed sense of momentum and enthusiasm
for her six-person graphic design company.

Tupper's firm produces award-winning work for an impressive array of
clients ranging from wineries to health care systems and technology companies. She and her staff produce memorable visual images, and she's very particular about the service provided by her firm, the work environment she
creates, and the reputation that results. During
her first seven years in business, she maintained *"We grow because we*
a loyal staff with little turnover. Thanks to the
dot-com boom with its frantic hiring and in-   *struggle, we learn*
flated salaries, she also survived a several-year   *and overcome."*
period during which she saw more than 20 staff
members come and go. That experience was the   R. C. ALLEN
source both of extreme stress and of dedication
to renewal. "I feel traumatized by the last several years," she says. "But we're
still here, and we have a greater number of clients, the majority of whom are
very, very happy. It was the skeleton beneath the business that needed repair."

Tupper started her firm as a one-person, home-based business in 1989 and
soon after hired her first employees: a part-time intern and a full-time multital-
ented staff member. "All three of us were in the upstairs bedroom," she remembers. "The living room was turned into a reception area, the dining room
turned into a conference room, and it got so crazy we finally moved the business out of the house."

Tupper maintained her group of three for another year, before a growing
client list prompted several additional full-time hires, bringing her staffing roster to about six—a number she considers near optimal to maintain the variety
of work and office atmosphere that is consistent with her vision. For a period of
several years, business was constant, client referrals increased, and employees
stayed with the firm for several years at a minimum. Then, in 1997, in the
midst of the dot-com frenzy, several longtime staff members left the firm, starting a rumbling that would become a several-year avalanche.

"It's been very awkward for me, because I've had to replace a lot of people in a relatively short period of time," Tupper says. "Half of those people left for legitimate reasons, like a spouse got transferred. But you have that many transitions and you think, 'Am I awful? Is my business terrible?'"

Tupper, intent on maintaining the same level of projects and staffing, started what has seemed like a nonstop recruitment effort. Looking for staff members who are dedicated, creative, and professional and fit with the firm's small, highly creative and service-oriented organizational culture, Tupper found herself with limited prospects and worse—designers who would accept a job only to leave for another employer in short order. "You do your best during the interview, and I've got an interview form and a list of questions I ask, and I wouldn't hire anyone who didn't seem like a good match," she says. "Yet I'd list four ads over a period of four weeks and get little in response. On paper, candidates would seem appropriate for an interview, but would arrive with green hair and a bone in their nose, which isn't an image my clients would find acceptable."

Tupper persisted in her recruitment efforts, replacing individuals who left and working nearly around the clock herself, despite having a toddler and a baby on the way in the middle of her staffing crisis. When the situation seemed endless and both her energy and resolve had started to wane, Tupper got a boost in the form of several former employees who returned to help her stem the flow and get the business back on stable ground. "It felt spiritual in nature," Tupper says of the return of her first full-time employee at a time when she was most needed. Two other former employees, one who had been with the firm for five years and left to become a freelance designer, another who had worked part-time while going to school, also returned for temporary stints, allowing Tupper to craft a turnaround strategy and begin to stabilize the staffing situation.

With the help of her team, Tupper put together what she called her October Plan, which called for a reorganization of the 10-year-old business. As part of the program, Tupper and her employees would be reviewing and updating everything from technology systems to client lists and floor designs. For Tupper, a self-described antichange freak, the overhaul was not easy. "I don't like change, and that's not a good quality for a small-business owner. I can be fully aware that things need to happen and put them on the back burner. So, in this situation, I was very lucky," says Tupper about having the assistance of a former employee who was more objective and less reticent about pointing out what needed to be overhauled.

"Having worked with me for several years at the start of this business, she knows I don't like change, I know I can trust her, and we both know that change is necessary right now for our growth. In reviewing everything, we found all sorts of things that hadn't been done properly. I'm just unloading cash on new people, new furniture, new technology. I'm looking at what's wrong, and I'm changing it."

To keep her focus on the highest priorities, Tupper also had to learn to delegate activities over which she'd maintained control. "I'm delegating administrative tasks that I'd held onto because I like to have control," she says. "But I looked at it and saw that by holding onto those tasks so tightly, I ultimately didn't have control at all. It's killing me not to butt in and get focused on [office management details]. It shouldn't matter to me, but it does. But I'm encouraging my staff to fix what's broken and letting them do what they need to do. That's all part of the plan."

While staff members implement the administrative and operational transformation, Tupper gives her attention to business development, client service, and of course, recruitment and employee management. "I've had interviews with existing staff members too," she says, "to discuss the changes and make sure they're happy here. They've committed to riding out this wave, even though it means working extra hours; and in return, I'm remunerating them with extra vacation and other perks."

Tupper also found that her staffing crisis, aside from being the catalyst for a thorough spring cleaning, brought her face-to-face with her original vision. "I started the business to have freedom, and that backfired. I found myself a slave to my business," she remembers. "When I started, I was completely unencumbered, so working until two o'clock in the morning was fine. That was okay and rewarding then; it invigorated me. Now I've got two small children, and I'm pooped." Tupper's October Plan was created, she says, to renew the business and to help create some balance between the demands of business ownership and the other priorities in her life. "I want to make sure the business doesn't collapse if I'm not here, and right now it does. My goal is to balance it out so I can have the flexibility, the freedom for which I started the business."

"It's tough," she continues. "We've got a lot going on right now, and a lot changing. But it's also very exciting. We're updating technology, changing our floor plan, referring inappropriate business or smaller accounts, celebrating 12 years in business, and revisiting our founding vision. We're really streamlining, and there's a lot coming to fruition."

Emergence: The Journey of Ummelina International Day Spa

Although containing quantitative growth is the perfect choice for some small-business owners while a larger business is more appropriate for others, there are times when a business owner finds that, through deliberate expansion, her vision unfolds and the business blossoms. While she may ultimately choose to cap quantitative growth, a certain amount of expansion allows the business to find its optimal size for manifesting her vision. Such was the case of Nina Ummel, whose Ummelina International Day Spa has more than doubled its payroll, from 25 to over 50 employees, and quadrupled its square footage since her 1998 decision to move to a new location and expand services.

"The key to growth is the introduction of higher dimensions of consciousness into our awareness."

PIR VILAYAT KHAN

Ummel graduated from college intent on teaching inner-city children, a desire that took her from her Indiana farm home to Seattle. When offered positions in Washington's rural areas, she decided that she'd have to create other options for her livelihood. Since her grandmother was an herbalist, her father a farmer, and her sibling an entrepreneur, Ummel decided to parlay her interest in skin-care, wellness, and education into a career, and ultimately her own business. After five years of work in other salons, Ummel launched her own three-person salon, Ummelina Day Spa, in 1986.

"It was clear to me that the direction everyone was taking in skin care was different from what I envisioned," says Ummel. "I had started using natural products, essential oils, and aromatherapy, which wasn't even talked about then. And there were no happy, soothing environments that supported that approach, so I decided to create my own."

After 10 years, Ummel found herself at a fork in the road: to maintain her business as it was, with about 20 employees in an increasingly cramped space and a resulting inability to take on additional clients, or to expand the business into a larger space that would accommodate a wider client base. She chose to expand. "It was a real debate. For 10 years, I had this little space and got to the point where I felt my wings were clipped. We just couldn't grow anymore. I saw expansion as a way to polish my gem," says Ummel. "I debated whether to stay fairly small, because I was concerned about finding enough high-quality, qualified employees required for an expanded business. Instead, I decided to have more space to allow people to move freely, create an environment, and allow more treatments. I opted to look for new space and grow."

· EXPANSION CHALLENGES

As is the case for many business owners who choose to expand their business, Ummel faced challenges that preceded her staff recruitment concerns: finding an appropriate commercial space and gaining the financing required for her plan. She spent two years searching for a new location in Seattle's increasingly tight commercial real-estate market; while she searched for space, leasing costs in the city tripled.

"It came down to four months before my lease was up, and I still didn't have a space," she remembers. "I couldn't look for a space on the street level, not for a service business. My ideal was to have my retail area at street level and my services either upstairs or down below street level. But every time I'd find a space, the big guys, the national chains, would come in and just blow away my offer. No matter how much the landlord liked me or my concept, the chains seemed like a more secure choice to them."

Ummel finally found a space two streets from her original location, but financing remained a challenge. While she ultimately obtained an SBA loan, the search wasn't an easy one. "Even though I felt very established in Seattle, with 10 years of experience and success with my business, the bankers really didn't understand what a spa did," she says. "I really had to take them by the hand, take them through the business, show them the figures, explain what we did."

The larger banks in the city continued to deny her loan applications—even the bank with which she had a 10-year relationship.
"They told me that they might consider it if I had a manufacturing
business, but not for the spa," recalls Ummel. At another bank,
Ummel was told that the small business department was really just
a hand-holding operation for minorities and women while those
parties looked for another source of funding. At yet another bank,
the loan officer told her they didn't understand her business and
wouldn't take the chance. Ummel was finally referred to a more
community-oriented bank branch that might better understand the
needs of her small business.

"I had to go outside of the city to find a loan," she says. "So it was almost a matter of what philosophy the bank had, with many of the
city bank branches being larger as a result of mergers and having
offices 25 floors above the street. There was a big difference, for me,
between the community bank and the big, downtown corporate
bank. The bank was used to loaning money to small businesses,
and didn't need all the protocol that the larger bankers required.
Large, urban banks just didn't understand small business, and they
just didn't get what a service business was about."

From a financial perspective, the expansion was more expensive
than Ummel anticipated. "The cost of moving, settling in, finding
the right employees, training people—it took more money and
more time," she says. She found that costs expanded beyond the
obvious, due to inefficiencies following the move and while the
company was growing. In addition, making financial projections
for the business was completely different since she could no longer
use historical, pre-expansion numbers to project future costs. She
also found that, due to higher costs for space, her profit margins
decreased.

A neighboring hot-dog stand proved to be one of Ummel's frustra-
tions at the spa's new address, primarily because the smell of boil-
ing hot dogs was incompatible with the environment she was trying
to create. The owner of the stand was supposed to have vacated the
spot prior to her arrival, and she was to have had that space as part
of her lease. But the hot dog vendor stayed. Ummel and her group,
trying to make light of a challenging situation, nicknamed the business Spa Dogs. But less than one year after moving to the new loca-

tion, she found herself faced with a surprise—and another challenge. The hot-dog vendor suddenly relinquished the space, forcing her to assume responsibility for the extra square footage or risk having an even more aromatic neighbor. She signed another lease, expanding her square footage, and her risk, well beyond her plan.

"Many people think that business owners are protected from financial misfortune if the company is incorporated, but you're not. You sign everything," says Ummel, referring to the risks business owners take in pursuit of their dreams. Like many of her peers, Ummel found the added risk level inspired her toward greater mastery. "Fortunately, I don't think I'm here to learn the effects of failure. That's a very powerful motivator!"

· THE MYTH OF MANAGED GROWTH

One of the things Ummel heard from her lender, among others, is that the quantitative growth she planned was fraught with peril. "People talked to me about managing growth, how that would be my biggest challenge, and I had no idea what they were talking about," she says. "Now I do. It's like a whole different business."

For Ummel, as for other business owners, quantitative growth challenges fall into several key categories: people, systems, and culture. First, in growing her staff from 20 to over 50 employees in eighteen months, Ummel noticed distinct changes in her employees and in her own role as the group's leader. "I've always loved change, and didn't realize that most people don't," she says. "There's a very clear disorientation that occurred, even in those very qualified employees, as a result of the move to a larger space and staff. We were so crammed in the old space, and now we look for people and can't find them! Everything was in a different place, so finding things was a challenge. Things just don't run as smoothly."

Ummel and her group had to adapt to the larger space and the growing staff and client roster while simultaneously creating new systems for working more efficiently in the revamped business model. Whereas they'd once used only two computers to run the business, they now had many computers, a new network, and new software that required working out a fair number of bugs. "Just the amount of time it takes to computerize functions that we'd been doing on paper has added to the challenge," she says. "We're very close to moving solely to the automated functions, but the biggest concern is that, with our scheduling and record keeping, that's where our money is. If it goes down without a backup, it'll kill us. So we've been duplicating computer and paper for six months until we're confident with the system."

Ummel also found that her familylike group, by doubling in size, had become more factionalized. "Former employees started regaling [new ones with] the good old days, and I noticed that, with people in positions of new responsibility, a more corporate structure started appearing, and people started worrying about who was above whom," she says. "I didn't want to allow that kind of work environment." So Ummel sought out a new vision of her organizational culture and found a new metaphor for Ummelina Day Spa: "It's a village now, a tribe instead of a family, and there are many families within the tribe. So that's how I'm running my business: not as a corporation, but as a tribe."

Having studied herbalism and tribal concepts, Ummel took a closer look at how tribes work and drew inspiration from that to find a new language and build a new culture at Ummelina. Treatment therapists became guides, reinforcing the experience of being taken on a journey at the spa. And Ummel adopted a circular, rather than hierarchical, structure. "It's a circle, rather than a pyramid," she explains. "Everyone is in the outer circle of guides, and we have an inner circle we call the Council. You have the chief and his or her council who have the decision-making responsibility within the tribe. And I created a group called scouts, who look ahead and scout out what's happening. The families within the tribe are divided up into different licensing areas or environments within the spa, and each family has its scout, who talks with the people within his particular group and brings any issues to the Council for discussion."

And the staff's response to this new cultural model? "Everyone comes in with this concept of the boss being at the top and all these people in between. They're programmed like that, whether from school, family, or other work environments where authority figures are the bad guys, the ones who tell you what to do," Ummel says. "So having to figure things out on their own and do them, sometimes that works better than other times. It just takes constant focus and attention, guidance all the time and reiterating that this is how we do things here."

Ummel says she learned a long time ago that not everyone is a right fit for her business. "Some people are better at understanding the concept and working within it than others, but that's what makes the decision of who should be here and who shouldn't," she says. "One of the pieces of advice I most remember when I was a new employer was from someone who said, 'Nina, you've planted your garden, and you have to weed it.' And you do. There are some people that have to be removed so others can grow and your garden is a healthy one. I know that the right employees only walk through the door when the door is open and other people have left, creating space for them."

To maintain a positive work environment and keep right-fit employees on staff, Ummel offers some standard benefits plus those that are unique to her environment. She offers free classes to employees and clients, and the former Spa Dog space has become a soothing Tea Spa that clients and staff members can use to relax, rejuvenate, host special events, and have educational conversations with the resident herbalist.

· FINDING SUPPORT DURING THE GROWTH SPURT

Ummel has an advisory council that includes one of her investors and a retired banker, and she meets in person or talks by phone with them when necessary. "They've been a tremendous support, sometimes just an emotional support when it gets really scary," she says. "Sometimes it's hard to remember what you've accomplished, which to other people seems pretty incredible. But to me, I'm still trying to create the best. So my advisers are good at reminding me what I've done and what's normal, since I can be very critical of my own business."

Ummel says she also gets support from employees, in the form of feedback on the work environment she's creating, and from her clients. "Hearing from our clients what Ummelina's done for them, what changes we've helped them make in their lives, and how much they enjoy coming in, how much healthier they are and how we're a part of their celebrations, that's a tremendous source of support,"

Ummel says. "So anytime it feels like it's overwhelming, just get around your clients more and listen!"

· MAKING THE CHOICE TO EXPAND

So what advice would Ummel pass along to other business owners considering quantitative growth for their companies? Not that it will be easy, and not that it's the only sure bet, but that each business owner has to follow his own heart.

"You have to be quiet enough to hear what you're really supposed to do. As business owners, we have the power to make those decisions," says Ummel. "We can ask ourselves whether we really want to take those risks to grow, how much more time we are willing to spend, and what kind of risks we're willing to take financially. In facing the decision, you learn what it's like to be an entrepreneur, that you have to know everything or learn everything, that you have to be willing to do it all, and that you have to sacrifice time that would otherwise go to other, often personal, things. You can easily lose a part of yourself."

"It would be easy, in growing as much as we have, for some people to feel desperate," Ummel continues, "where you get to the point where you have so many people asking for your services, and you need extra people to provide the services. But it's never a good idea to grow just because you're desperate, where you're hiring people who may not be right for your environment. It's better sometimes to call and reschedule clients so that when they do come in, they get the quality service that your reputation has been built on."

Creating a Personal Definition for Growth

In reviewing these stories, and others, about the choices business owners make regarding growth, we can see that there are advantages and disadvantages in staying compact and concentrated or choosing the path of expansion. Ultimately, the choice depends heavily on the vision and preferences of the business owner: what's most important to him, personally? What does she want her role to be? What's motivating him to add employees, clients, or space in the first place? What's most important about the business? What differentiates it from others? What's the relationship between the size of the business and its products or services?

The answers to these questions may evolve, too, with the business itself. At one point, it may be appropriate to contain the business's growth. Two years later, in response to new opportunities to add products or services, increased size may be required. Perhaps the most important action a business owner can take regarding growth is to free himself from the limitation of thinking that there's only one way and one time to grow and to adopt instead an appreciation for the evolutionary nature of the business and himself.

The rest of this book provides forays into three avenues for qualitative growth—vision, right relationship, and wisdom and mastery—that a big-vision small-business owner pursues to enhance the meaning and value of her journey and distinguish herself from both large-company and small-business peers.

KEY No 2:
TO LIVE LARGE,
YOU HAVE TO
VISION BIG

"WE NEVER KNOW

HOW HIGH WE ARE

TIL WE ARE CALLED TO RISE."

Emily Dickinson, No. 1176

"A VISION WITHOUT A TASK IS

A DREAM. A TASK WITHOUT A VISION

IS DRUDGERY. A VISION AND

A TASK IS THE HOPE OF THE WORLD."

Inscription in a church,

Sussex, England, c. 1730

Chapter 6

VISION IN THE SMALLEST ENTERPRISES

As a young man, mythologist Joseph Campbell reportedly wrote in his journal, "Business, as I have seen it so far, reduces living men to dull machines, that go on from day to day working at stupid tasks with not the slightest idea of what they're working for."[1] A big-vision small business requires a clear, inspiring, high-reaching vision that guides and sustains the big-vision business owner on his or her journey. But what does vision mean to this entrepreneur when it is compared to the standard and somewhat staid vision or mission statements that are routine in most organizations? How formal does the inspired-visioning process, and correlated planning, have to be so that the visionary small enterprise doesn't become "a dull machine"?

Visioning and planning can, at least to many small-business owners, seem the domain of large corporations, where legions of people are hired to do just that. In most corporations, vision statements tend to be simple descriptions of quantitative goals—with most being far from visionary. As for organizational planning, the traditional parameters often come from professors in university business schools who consult to large entrepreneurial ventures or multinational corporations. On the bookshelves of your local bookstore or library, many of the books on planning are geared to these larger companies and seem to carry an assumption that such big-company planning processes are appropriate for small enterprises as well. But most of these resources don't speak to the unique needs of the business comprised of two to thirty people. For big-vision small-business owners, traditional visioning and business plan models can seem uncomfortably similar to wearing an ill-fitting shoe.

Many small-business owners feel disconnected from the more formal visioning and planning processes that tend to be solely quantitative in focus. As a result, they may reject them outright or create vision statements and business plans that meet the criteria for obtaining financing but are otherwise devoid of meaning and inspiration. Why is that important? For several reasons, one being that we tend to bring into reality the very things we focus on most; so we need to be mindful of exactly what it is we're creating. This is particularly true if the business is a vehicle for service to the world. Also, a small business and its owner have a symbiotic relationship, meaning that an uninspired or out-of-control business often catches a business owner's motivation, mindset, and personal life in its undertow—and vice versa. An uninspired, burned-out business owner has an effect on the momentum of her enterprise.

Maintaining allegiance to high ideals, deeply held values, and a big-vision small-business sense of purpose and mission often adds to the usual rigors of small-business ownership. However, a clear vision and an aligned action plan that are inspired and dynamic enough to suit the evolving and more personalized small business, together serve as a guiding star when the seas are choppy— or when the seas seem so smooth we can easily be lulled into complacency.

"Each great human accomplishment begins with some kind of vision or dream," says Dr. JoAnn Dahlkoetter, author of *Your Performing Edge* and a San Carlos, California–based sports psychologist who has worked with elite athletes on peak performance and goal achievement. "There needs to be a hunger, a fire inside which fuels your passion to achieve an important goal, regardless of your ability level. Where the mind goes, everything else follows."[2] The same is true in business. Studies show that having a strong vision or purpose for a company and effectively engaging employees in achieving that mission are key traits of high-performing companies of all sizes, even more than having the proper processes and systems, though those are important as well.[3]

Ironically, despite the common practice of creating a vision statement in most corporations, being idealistic or having an inspired social purpose isn't something that is welcomed or appreciated in the traditional, money-driven business world. For example, being called a visionary is considered somewhat of an insult in California's venture capital–driven Silicon Valley, where financial return on investment—as big and rapidly as possible—is the primary interest. Bob Metcalf, inventor of Ethernet and founder of 3Com, confirmed as much in *Wired* magazine: "Nobody wants visionaries running companies." For an entrepreneur who wants to be taken seriously by investors looking for quantitative growth and high return on investment, Metcalf advised, "never let a publicist call you a visionary."[4]

Having high ideals and an inspired vision is often translated as not being focused enough on financial wealth building, an assumption held by many lenders who frown upon loans for service-oriented or social-purpose organizations. In a big-vision small business, however, with its emphasis on balancing quality of life and quantity of profit, ideals and vision provide both fuel and focus to the enterprise. Profits provide a means to finding ways to manifest the vision in the business's everyday reality.

So how can a big-vision small-business owner find a middle path between adopting stodgy processes borrowed from large corporations and rejecting the visioning and planning processes altogether? Begin now to forget everything you know or have heard about visioning and planning. Drop your preconceptions and allow yourself to experience what Buddhists call "the beginner's mind" or those on the Christian path might call "becoming like a child again." We're going to review potential priorities that are common to big-vision small businesses, formulate our own definitions, and consider creating an approach that is energizing yet realistic for an independent, creative, challenge-loving (or challenge-addicted), busy small-business owner.

The next chapter identifies 12 priorities that real-world big-vision small-business owners have identified as pathways to qualitative growth and contribution. Their choices about which priorities they emphasize depend largely on their own vision for their enterprise, as well as their skills, spiritual traditions, and lifestyle goals. The priorities lead into a broader discussion regarding definitions for vision, values, and mission in a big-vision enterprise; options for customizing visioning and planning approaches; and profiles that exhibit the place of an inspired vision and vision-into-action plan in real-world enterprises.

Chapter 7

Twelve Priorities of Big-Vision Small Businesses

Before moving into a discussion of what *vision* might mean in a big-vision small business, it's helpful to review some of the priorities that such owners have for their enterprises. The priorities speak to how the business owner wants others to experience his enterprise, how the organization affects the community or world at large, and what greater purpose the activities of the enterprise support. That the enterprise is small in size and more independent in ownership increases the likelihood that the priorities can be put into practice more deeply and sustainably in comparison to what's possible—and necessary—in a large firm that's more quantitative in focus.

Unlike many companies that seem to have a significant gap between espoused principles and actual decisions and effects, big-vision small-business owners may opt to limit quantitative growth, turn away a profitable account, or forego entry into a hot new market if it means casting aside their business's core values or the larger mission to which the enterprise contributes. Interviewees for this book aspired to some if not all of the following guiding principles in their day-to-day decision making.

Priority No. 1: Ensuring Mutual Benefit

An emerging trend in corporate America, one significant enough to be cited as one of "Six Principles of Business in the 21st Century" by *Civilization* magazine, is to make your customers work for you.[5] Consumers, in such a scheme, become so-called "prosumers" and are manipulated into assuming responsibility for beta-testing products and doing research and other tasks formerly handled by a company employee. Such disrespect for one's customer would be appalling to small-business visionaries. Yet this behavior seems to grow more common in boom times, when fast growth and short-term wealth accumulation become ever more blinding priorities.

Boom or bust, big-vision small-business owners aim to ensure that both they and those with whom they do business—whether employees, customers, or vendors—genuinely benefit from the interaction. "Each interaction should be for the highest good of the people involved. I try to ask, 'Is it in all of our best interests? What's your best interest? How well do I understand what someone else needs, and do they understand what I'm about?'" says Barb Banonis, founder of LifeQuest International in Charleston, West Virginia. "For me, my business is about fostering well-being on all levels."

Priority No. 2: Creating Right Livelihood

A term borrowed from Buddhism, *right livelihood* refers to our desire to do meaningful work, conducted in a mindful way, that contributes positively to the community or at least does no harm. The concept of right livelihood can be more readily applied in a small enterprise, where the heart and soul of the owner infuses the way the business operates, thus becoming the heart and soul of the business. Why?

In a big-vision small business, the enterprise owner is often the sole or major investor and is able to make decisions that are deemed less profitable, and therefore unacceptable, in a large firm with higher overhead, more investors, and a greater hunger for quantitative performance and return on investment. The big-vision small-business owner, in collaboration with others on her team who are passionate about right livelihood, redefines priorities in a way that generates a higher rate of qualitative return on investment, along with the quantitative performance necessary to fund those higher priorities.

"There are only so many hours in a week, and we spend a third of that sleeping. We have to make the rest of it count," says Christopher Adamo, founder of

Zen Myotherapy Massage and Oasis Onsite in San Francisco. "Instead, we commiserate—misery loves company! But we hoard our joy. In right livelihood, we share the joy."

Eileen Spitalny, cofounder of Chandler, Arizona–based Fairytale Brownies, did just that, when she and her partner took their joy for after-school brownies and turned it into a small business with national distribution and a product that earned recognition in the *Wall Street Journal*. "I love seeing people get so excited about the brownies," says Spitalny. "It's just so much fun, and brownies are just so harmless."

Priority No. 3: Fostering Right Relationships

Big-vision small-business owners place a high value on relationships, not just as an image-boosting gimmick but out of a deep respect for others, whether employees, customers, vendors, or in the case of Ellen Kruskie in Raleigh, North Carolina, the furry beneficiaries of her efforts. Kruskie, founder of Carolina PetSpace, a pet wash and products store, provides supplies and services that ultimately help people create more respectful, rewarding relationships with the animals in their care. "Taking care of animals is serious business. Pets are not accessories; you don't put them on a shelf when you want to go away for the weekend," she says. "They're living, sentient creatures for whom we have a responsibility." Her passion for honoring the relationships between animals and their humans, as much as her interest in entrepreneurship, moved her to create Carolina PetSpace.

Other big-vision small-business owners take relationships with other people just as seriously. Iris Harrell, founder of Harrell Remodeling in Menlo Park, California, has a commitment to respectful relationships that permeates the workplace and her company's relationships with customers. "I don't see employees as pieces of wood to discard when I don't need them," Harrell says. "Others look at 'the labor pool' rather than John Smith, father and future vice president." Contrary to the norms in the construction industry, Harrell Remodeling sets itself apart by demonstrating respect for people in its commitment to providing full-time employment with benefits and making sure that customers don't have to endure noise, foul language, and litter, to name a few of the less pleasant things that are common to most construction sites.

In larger enterprises, the push for maximized financial return on investment renders the time and care required for deeper right-relationship practices unprofitable, though individuals or small groups of employees can always choose such practices to guide their own behavior. In an average small business, the tenets of right relationship are too demanding or troublesome and are thus not often a high priority. In a big-vision small business, right-relationship practices add meaning and maximize a potential strength of small enterprise. For big-vision small-business owners, right relationship offers a way to increase personal mastery or practice spiritual tenets in a way that also benefits the enterprise and its stakeholders. For a more in-depth discussion of right-relationship practices in a big-vision small enterprise, see Section Three.

PRIORITY NO. 4: GIVING BACK
TO THE COMMUNITY

Whether being available to new business owners, doing pro bono work, donating to local causes, or choosing to work with charitable organizations that might not have the budgets of a for-profit organization, big-vision small-business owners make a commitment to giving back to the community. Such practices stem from a generosity of spirit and a goal of making a positive contribution, as well as from a desire to balance quality of life with quantity of profit. In a small enterprise, an owner can more readily sustain such commitments out of a personal belief in their importance, even when such a commitment reduces the potential financial profit margin.

Helen Hempstead, of Cor Productions, a St. Louis, Missouri, video production company, says that she and her partners do most of their work for nonprofits, many of which are religious organizations, though corporate video projects are much more lucrative financially. "Some of the promotional videos we do, particularly for religious orders, involve going and staying in those communities," she says, "so you really develop a sense for what it's like. It gives our work meaning." Hempstead says their work with nonprofits is often comforting to the corporations with whom they do work: "Corporations look at our work for nonprofits and think, 'If you do this type of work, I can trust you.'"

Other business owners, such as Bruce Hetrick of Hetrick Communications, a public relations firm in Indianapolis, strive to work with clients whose products or services contribute to a healthier world. "We don't have a lot of clients who make and sell widgets," says Hetrick. "Every client is in some way good for society, good for people. In my career, I've increased the use of safety belts, increased the use of condoms to prevent AIDS. I don't know whose life I've helped save or who's healthier because of it, but it feels good knowing that we're in some way contributing to a better world."

The smaller the group, the truer the saying: Time is money. Each of these commitments cuts into potential revenue generation, which, due to the group's small size, can't be made up by coworkers as easily as a large enterprise can. Pro bono work, compensated volunteer time, direct contributions—all create costs paid by the enterprise, and would be immediate candidates for cost cutting if the sole focus was quantitative return on investment. Since big-vision small-business owners define contribution and return-on-investment in both qualitative and quantitative terms, such social investments are critical to fulfilling the enterprise's vision and mission.

Priority No. 5: Aspiring toward High Ethical Ground

Many big-vision small-business owners place a high premium on creating a business that's known as being highly ethical and trustworthy. Whether that means admitting a mistake, compensating employees fairly, paying your taxes and other bills on time, or turning away business for which you're not optimally suited, a business known for its ethics is built on a series of consistently honest transactions. In an era wrought with news of ethics breaches in large companies—the Enron scandal is but one example—holding to an ideal of integrity in daily business transactions can no longer be assumed for large or small business.

Business owner Bill Hayes says that creating a business based on integrity is a high priority for him. Based in Boulder, Colorado, Hayes founded his printing company and recently merged with another, creating Estey Printing. Since the firm he bought had a poor credit rating, Hayes found himself dealing with longtime suppliers who wouldn't deliver to the newly purchased business. "It's incredible to me, the companies that don't pay their bills," says Hayes. "We'd dealt with this supplier for 15 years, and they said they'd deliver to us knowing that I had bought the company. I'd never want someone to say I didn't pay my bills." On a practical level, Hayes's reputation for integrity has helped him with such things as getting financing and quickly resolving issues with the Internal Revenue Service.

Other big-vision small-business owners practice their commitment to high ethical standards by turning away lucrative opportunities because the actions of the potential client company conflict with priorities for public health, cultural or environmental sustainability, and other social-responsibility interests.

Priority No. 6: Creating a Respectful Environment

Owners of visionary small businesses are driven to create good work environments, using past experience or spiritual beliefs as guides to what they would or would not do in their own workplace. For some, like Nina Ummel of Ummelina International Day Spa in Seattle or Jessie Zapffe of Golden Bough Books in Mount Shasta, California, this translates to creating a beautiful, nurturing environment for employees and customers. Zapffe has done that by selecting a soothing décor for her bookstore and offering an inventory that is visually attractive while supporting well-being and spiritual development. Her store looks and feels like a sacred space.

Like Zapffe, Ummel wanted to create a gentle atmosphere for her spa that fosters relaxation and rejuvenation; she shares more details in an in-depth profile in Section One. For other big-vision small-business owners, a respectful workplace incorporates the practice of right relationship by encouraging a participatory environment, offering creative benefits or flexible scheduling, ensuring family-friendly policies, or providing a relaxing oasis for clients who stop by.

Cec Stanford, founder of Prairie Herb Company in Gillette, Wyoming, wanted to create a business that produced superior-quality specialty vinegars while remaining family friendly. As a result, she offers both flexibility and her

understanding so that her employees never feel like th

tween taking care of a sick child or keeping their job. "I ha

was faced with a dilemma if someone got sick. You worry a

ford. "I was determined that if I ever had employees, they v

about something so essential as taking care of their families. (

fold: producing excellent products and nurturing good relations,

Priority No. 7: Generating Reveni a Means Rather Than the Primary (

In our culture, the dominant worldview holds that we're in business t much money as possible; the more of it we make, the more success considered. That's supposed to be our primary goal, and questions abc companies usually begin with "how many" or "how much." The leader in vision small business certainly pursues financial well-being but not franti or blindly and not at the expense of the inspired vision and core operating v ues. The numerical bottom line is but one aspect of operational effectiveness the numbers are a means by which the enterprise can be a reliable vehicle for contribution and quality of life.

With this in mind, a visionary owner works thoughtfully and diligently to find a healthy balance between his firm's social mission and the need to generate adequate revenue to support the organization's work and the quality of life for both leader and employees. The larger the organization and the more it is driven by maximized return to a larger group of investors, the more likely it is that socially responsible activities become servants in the quest to produce higher financial returns rather than existing as part of the organization's primary purpose.

On a more global scale, seeking that balance stems from deeply held beliefs about the very role of business and our economic system. Mike Sheldrake, owner of Polly's Gourmet Coffee in Long Beach, California, says that many small-business owners with whom he comes into contact have problems finding that balance. "Everyone seems to want to go into business for emotional reasons," Sheldrake says. "Either they're enamored with the industry, or they love their product, or they hate their current job. But if they don't know their numbers and what they want to make each month, they have a hobby, not a

ess. Ideally, you have to have both the passion for your product and a han-
n your books."

For me it's a humanistic philosophy," says Jim Amaral, founder of Borealis
ads of Wells, Maine. "The economy and business are there for the people,
the other way around. Ultimately, the business has to benefit the people in-
lved. If it's exploiting people in order to maintain the business, it's not a
ealthy business."

PRIORITY NO. 8: FOSTERING
HEALTH AND WELLNESS

Whether literally or figuratively, many big-vision small-business owners envision their product, service, or work approach as fostering greater health and
wellness in their world. For Debra and Ron Herrsche of Westhampton Chiro-
practic in Richmond, Virginia, and Karen Straight of Knead For Life Neuromuscular Therapy in Raleigh, North Carolina, helping people get and stay
healthy is a primary purpose of their holistic health-care organizations. For
Golden Bough Books' Zapffe, the business promotes healing and wellness
through its product inventory and atmosphere. "A lot of people need nurturing," she says. "They're either working with computers or they're alienated
from other people. So I really tried to create a space that's very nurturing for
people who come in the store."

The controversy over so-called "corporate healthcare"—with physicians and
nurses expressing concern that patient health and well-being is being sub-
verted in the push for maximized efficiency and profit—is a good example of
how the ideals for promoting wellness can fall under attack as financial return
on investment becomes the primary operating requirement. In an independently owned, big-vision small enterprise, health and well-being are qualitative
return-on-investment priorities even when sustaining the practices cuts into
the potential profit margin.

PRIORITY NO. 9: PROMOTING AWARENESS
AND PERSONAL RESPONSIBILITY

Some big-vision small-business owners endeavor to cultivate greater levels of
personal responsibility and, often above and beyond the operating necessities

of their business, try to raise awareness to that end. Carolina PetSpace's Kruskie, for example, stocks and reviews carefully selected books and sees herself as an information conduit, sharing knowledge about responsible animal care and encouraging discussion among her customers.

For Sheldrake of Polly's Gourmet Coffee, promoting awareness and self-responsibility can sometimes mean the difference between surviving the entry of a big-chain competitor or not. On one hand, Sheldrake has seen several small, privately owned businesses in his Long Beach shopping district fold after the arrival of competing chain stores. He, on the other hand, viewed the new competition as an impetus to take responsibility and refine his operating model, an experience he shares in Section Four.

Other big-vision small-business owners might cultivate an internal environment that runs on individual responsibility, where employees have a greater than usual share of both the rewards and risks in operating the enterprise. This internal mission of personal responsibility might include employee-created job descriptions and even employee-driven performance reviews—in which the employees take responsibility for defining their roles and goals, gaining agreement from their employer, and seeking feedback on their performance. In larger organizations, there is more of a shift from personal to organizational responsibility, and human resource rules and processes are dictated by a division charged with enforcing the company's policies, which leaves less room for individual expression or experimentation.

Priority No. 10: Cultivating Conscious-Business Practices

Thanks to their reputation for agility and experimentation, small businesses can be vehicles for changing the very way business is done, as advocates of conscious and socially responsible business emphasize. And some big-vision small enterprises with an outwardly focused social mission are created for the purpose of fostering social or cultural transformation.

Whether driven by the big-vision small-business owner's own humanistic philosophy or spiritual traditions or not, doing conscious work promotes—or is at least openly respectful of—values such as tolerance, compassion, sustainability, community, environmental stewardship, and respecting the dignity of all beings. In a larger corporation, socially responsible ideals may be offset by less mindful or outright damaging practices, thus minimizing or even negating the net impact of the company's very worthwhile social-responsibility programs. Again, because big-vision small businesses are independently owned and small in size, such practices are more likely to fully infuse the organization's way of operating and result in a more positive net impact.

This is the case with Melinda Moulton, one of two sustainability-focused partners in Burlington, Vermont–based Main Street Landing. "We want to make a change in the way business happens and the way construction is done and people build buildings," says Moulton. "My business card says, 'We're not your typical developer.' We've received a lot of recognition for simply being different in what we do."

For Dagmer Chew, owner of Homestead Real Estate Co. in Cape May, New Jersey, ushering in a new way of working led to what is considered blasphemy in the real-estate business: closing her shop on Sundays so her employees could spend time with their families, go to church, or observe other sacred rituals.

PRIORITY NO. 11: SETTING HIGH STANDARDS FOR QUALITY

Whether pertaining to right relationship, personal mastery, or conscious enterprise, many big-vision small-business owners opt for self-employment so they're able to do their work according to the high standard they believe they and their stakeholders deserve. In this way, they're more like the master craftsmen of old than they are disciples of mass production. Shelby Putnam Tupper, founder of Shelby Designs & Illustrates in Oakland, California, is another embodiment of this concept. Tupper is determined to offer the highest quality work regardless of the client's revenue category. "I see many other firms, many of them big and well-known, who'll assign interns to pro bono accounts and send out swill for a product," says Tupper. "Everything we do, whether it's free or high budget, looks great. We might require flexibility on timelines for pro bono accounts, but neither quality nor care nor service slack."

As Keith Rollins, the Portland, Maine–based entrepreneur, confirmed, highly refined standards for right relationship, service, or quality are more easily met in a big-vision small enterprise than they are in a large organization whose first priority is investor returns. Whereas larger enterprises can excel at mass-production and broad distribution, small enterprises with a conscious focus can easily surpass large-company norms for personalized relationship, quality, and service.

Priority No. 12: Connecting Business and Spiritual Practices

For some people, unifying work with one's spiritual or religious life is the ideal goal to be achieved, and running a small business seems a perfect vehicle through which to serve others and refine one's own spiritual practice or apply wisdom gained from the contemplative life to the more practical tasks of the active life.

We often hear of Mary Kay Cosmetics and Service Master as examples of companies where the spiritual principles of the founder are deeply ingrained in the organization's core values. Yet there are countless other businesses, perhaps smaller and less known, that serve as fertile ground for practices drawn from the owner's spiritual foundation. Remember, for example, Dagmer Chew's New Jersey real estate firm that closed its offices on Sunday.

"Where there is no vision, the people perish."

Proverbs 29:18

And then there is Marc Lesser, whose California company, Brush Dance, sells greeting cards, journals, and other products that feature spiritual messages. Lesser's vision and leadership style are influenced by his Zen Buddhist training and his tenure as executive director of the Tassajara monastery before he decided to start Brush Dance. As emphasized in the company's marketing materials, the very name of the company communicates the vision: "The Brush Dance is a Yurok Indian healing ritual where being true to yourself means giving your best to help a person in need." Lesser envisions his company as one in which right livelihood, right relationship, and positive impact are operational norms experienced by everyone who comes into contact with the organization.

Big-Vision Priorities and Business Norms

To some, these principles may seem ordinary in today's politically correct world, where the media is full of talk about socially responsible business and socially conscious undertakings are a crucial element of corporate image campaigns. An assumption that responsible practices are the norm in business, however, confuses public relations campaigns with the actual net impact when all of a company's activities are reviewed and averaged.

If we look beneath the advertising hype and public relations spin, we too often see a wide gulf between rhetoric and action. For example, a study released in June 2000 by the Ethics Resource Center in Washington, D.C., showed a growing number of employees who say corporate integrity is as important to them as income, but about one-third of those surveyed said they'd observed misconduct at work, and almost half were fearful of reporting the unethical behavior. A study released at about the same time by the consulting firm KPMG found that 7 of 10 employees witnessed unethical conduct in the workplace.[6] And that was before the Enron debacle, which showed that a culture of greed and questionable ethics ultimately revealed itself in a company that had only just before the implosion been lauded for its "good corporate citizenship" and touted as one of the best companies to work for.[7]

An April 2000 report in *The Economist* suggested that corporate ethics activities, such as growing trends for appointing an ethics officer or providing ethics training, were motivated more by a desire to avoid public relations fiascoes and costly regulation than by altruism. And, further distinguishing big-vision small enterprises and other small businesses, the same article reported that "small firms, in particular, pay far less attention than bigger rivals to normalizing ethical issues and to worrying about their social responsibilities."[8]

So the commitment of big-vision small businesses to such high principles may be all the more admirable. After all, their tight, often bootstrap budgets, carefully allocated resources, and fewer personnel regulatory requirements could offer a perfectly legitimate excuse to avoid such potentially expensive and time-consuming operating philosophies. Instead, big-vision owners take on, and even enjoy, the challenge of shepherding their visionary ideals and ethical principles into action while tackling the more mundane operational issues common to small-business ownership.

Pursuing Big-Vision Values while Meeting Real-World Challenges

Achieving a balance between lofty values and an inspired vision, on one hand, and the day-to-day reality of running a business, on the other, is no easy feat. Doing so requires total commitment to visionary guiding principles, even when it would be easier, cheaper, and perhaps even acceptable as the norm, in the short term, to opt solely for personal gain, to maximize our investment, to do the minimum required for our employees and customers, to limit the quality of our product or service to the minimum the market would accept, and to settle comfortably into the status quo.

This is perhaps the real distinguishing factor of the big-vision small-business owner, who has multiple bottom lines and chooses The Work, service and qualitative growth, over expediency or short-term material gain. In doing so, she allows her business to sand away her rough edges and refine her ability to serve her family, employees, customers, and community and, through them and with her like-minded colleagues, the world.

With these priorities in mind and heart, the big-vision small-business owner relies upon a clear, inspiring vision to be his anchor or guiding star, depending on what the circumstances require. The next chapters offer a discussion of what *vision, mission,* and *values* mean; how to refresh and clarify the guiding vision; and finally how to bridge the vision with the day-to-day decisions and behaviors of all in the organization so that the ideals of the big-vision enterprise move further from myth and closer to reality.

Chapter 8

THE GUIDING VISION

IF WE HAVE A CLEAR IDEA but it stems solely from external success factors or advice, we may very well end up with a seemingly successful business that we aren't passionate about or a business that never takes off for the same lack of passion. If our vision is murky or misplaced, then the results tend to be so as well. In a big-vision small enterprise, a misaligned or unclear vision is a drag on the motivation and inspiration that's needed to propel a group past mediocrity and into the extraordinary. Creating a clear, inspiring vision—and revisiting it as often as necessary—provides a solid foundation from which to launch the enterprise's activities, or to which we can return when confusion rules the day and we need that grounding in our original guiding vision.

As do many who endeavor to create a big-vision small enterprise, I know this only too well from my own experience as the founder of Ivy Sea, Inc., a boutique organizational consulting firm that specializes in helping clients create sustainable practices for inspired leadership, respectful communication, and more effective ways of working together.

With a talent for visioning, planning, and implementing what I plan, I created a business that was, by all appearances, everything my advisers and colleagues said it should be: busy and quantitative in focus, with zero debt, a well-appointed office in what would become a trendy neighborhood, eight or so people, a growing and impressive client list, strong revenues, better than average profit margins, and solid, well-researched plans for more, more, more. The problem? I had created a quantitatively focused enterprise and was increasingly cognizant of the difference between that and a big-vision small business. I didn't feel particularly good about all of the work we were doing; it seemed obvious to me that some of our client companies had no real interest in respectful, effective communication that served those working in and otherwise affected by the companies.

What's more, I realized that I'd created a team that, though it included terrific and talented people, was more appropriate to the current state of the business than what I had envisioned it could and should be. I followed the line from the picture-perfect business plan to the future it would lead to and decided it wasn't someplace I wanted to work, much less work at creating. After five years of quantitatively successful entrepreneurship, I started dreading Monday and found myself wondering when and how, given the time, energy, and care I had put into creating the business, that had happened.

"If our vision is murky or misplaced, then the results in the business tend to be so as well."

That's a pretty sobering day, when the distance between where you thought you were headed, where you are, and where you want to be seems as if it couldn't be greater; and the very thought of moving away from a business model to which you've devoted money, time, and energy and that is so highly regarded by others—people whom you respect and from whom you want respect—seems not just fraught with risk but downright stupid. Regardless, I and my colleagues were determined to change course and navigate our way through an organizational transformation from a quantitatively successful entrepreneurial firm to a qualitatively effective big-vision small enterprise. In committing to the evolution of the firm, we experienced both challenges and successes, as you'll see. Even with the hurdles and the costs, the visioning and redirecting we did from that day on led us through the evolution of InnoVision Communication to Ivy Sea, Inc. I enjoy my business again, and we are energized each time we revisit our vision and plans for the future. And there have been days when that's no easy task.

Here in the San Francisco Bay Area, during a five-year period of frenzied obsession with dot-com startups and initial public offerings (IPOs), the lure of moving to an e-commerce business plan and courting venture capital was incredibly compelling. On some days, the temptation was so strong I'd have to leave the office and spend a few hours walking or at a spa or movie theater to refocus, or simply sit in meditation or prayer until the urge to leap onto the e-bandwagon passed. As I discussed this with trusted colleagues or business advisers during a recent meeting, one adviser asked me why I didn't do it. A good question, particularly given our journey from quantitative focus to qualitative enterprise. The truth is, while the myth of the instant e-millionaire tempted like the Devil in the desert, the place it beckoned me to is, in my mind, desertlike. Greed, in itself, did not prove a compelling enough vision—not just for me but for the many startup enterprises that ultimately fell flat when funding ran out and there was no prevailing idea or vision to motivate its people or propel the venture through the twin crises of funding and purpose. Greed is not a sustainable source of motivation. Knowing that, and remembering the turnaround we at Ivy Sea had only recently completed, guided us back on course when we were buffeted by external forces, such as well-publicized models of mainstream success in our profit-before-everything culture. To find our way to that sense of equilibrium and clarity, we followed the same ideal, faced the same array of challenges, and tapped the very practices that I share throughout this book.

What is that ideal? For a big-vision small business, it is to do well enough financially by doing something that's gratifying to those within the organization and truly good, in some way, for the local community or the world. And good, in a big-vision enterprise, goes beyond a periodic, thought-free donation or providing a product or service that does nothing other than encourage people to move faster, spend more, reflect less, eat while driving, talk while eating, work while vacationing, and the like. The world doesn't need more of business as usual.

Yet it's also optimal to me, as with other big-vision small-business owners, to make enough money by doing something I love in a way that makes a positive, healthy contribution to the world. That we're meeting a need, or giving people what they want, or not breaking any laws doesn't necessarily mean that what we're doing is right or good or ethical or healthy. And for many of the big-vision small-business owners with whom I spoke, that's not good enough. The ideal vision is to marry a healthy humanistic bottom line with a healthy financial one. Creating a right-vision small business that's financially healthy is incredibly difficult, as many such idealist-visionaries can tell you, especially if the business is something other than product manufacturing and the definition of right business goes beyond donating a portion of profits to charitable organizations. Since smaller, privately owned enterprises can be both more agile and independent, experimenting with and exploring the depths of big-vision, right-relationship options and opportunities is more feasible than it is for a larger, investor-driven, quantitatively focused business.

> *"The leisure-society is actually a nightmare because in reality it's the self-indulgence society, the filling-time society, the killing-time society, the 'Why am I here?' society—with no purpose."*
>
> Ian Garrett,
> Jesmond Parish Church

With this in mind, viewing the big-vision small business as a multifaceted journey is an asset. More important even than what we do as big-vision small-business owners is why we do it, and then how. The *what* may or may not happen; the need for *why*—as in "Why am I doing this?"—will most certainly make itself abundantly clear at various points along your journey. This is why taking the time to reflect and vision, and then translating that vision into an action plan, is crucial.

How Does Vision Differ from Mission and Core Values?

The terms *vision, mission,* and *core values* have become old from overuse and are often used interchangeably, so a good place to start a visioning process is to make sure we know what we mean by these words. For the purposes of our discussion about big small-business vision, let's assume the following definitions:

Vision. There are several good definitions of vision offered by the *Random House Webster's College Dictionary,* particularly "the act or power of anticipating that which will or may come to be"; "something seen in or as if in a dream or trance, often attributed to divine agency"; or "a vivid, imaginative conception or anticipation."[9] In many stock market–driven or quantitatively focused organizations, a vision statement is put together as if participants are sleepwalking through the process with no real intention of allowing the vision to transform their own behavior and thus the behavior and destiny of the company.

Chiseling a vision statement that summarizes a quantitative goal is very different from reflecting on visionary possibilities and articulating them in a thoughtfully crafted summary that guides the enterprise toward affecting some corner of the world in a positive way. In many companies, if you read through the pleasant jargon, vision or mission statements come down to one clear purpose of the organization: maximizing return to the company's major investors. As mentioned earlier, visionary enterprise includes qualitative as well as quantitative goals and is thus less likely when the one true goal is increasing revenues for maximum financial returns. Whether this is good or bad depends on your perspective; to me, it's simply a reality in larger organizations, particularly those that have publicly traded stock, where the owners are greater in number and care primarily about a return on their investment rather than the enterprise's social mission.

"We have to describe for the world what this new society will look like. What we currently have is a president saying, 'We are going to root out terrorism and keep shopping.' That is not a vision to me. We need truly visionary leaders who can help direct the inner strength of the people."

REV. DR. MICHAEL BECKWITH, *UTNE READER* (JANUARY–FEBRUARY 2002)

In our big-vision small businesses, the guiding vision should be a picture of reality at its most optimal—a reality that through our work we help in some way, however small, to bring out. A picture that is vivid and imaginative: something we and, we hope, others would anticipate eagerly as a positive and qualitative contribution to the world, or our corner of it. Our vision should be inspired, uncensored by the norms, limitations, and expectations of others. Our vision is what we would create in our most perfect imaginings of what should be possible in the world, and it informs our behavior so that it does, indeed, become possible. In a big-vision small enterprise, the vision goes well beyond simple financial performance, though financial health is a necessary factor for supporting the firm's work.

Mission. Though inspired by vision, mission is more task oriented. Our mission summary answers the question "If this is our grand vision for our contribution to the world, then what is our practical, day-to-day work to help bring that about?" If our vision was, for example, a world in which no one went hungry, our mission might be to identify locations and causes of hunger, to teach community-specific sustainable farming techniques, or to help teach skills that help unemployed individuals transition to self-sustaining employment. If our vision was to make knowledge accessible to the masses, regardless of class or caste, then our mission might be to create and distribute a high-quality, easy-to-use computer and help connect public libraries and schools to the Internet. If our vision was a world of collaboration and tolerance, our mission might be to foster heightened awareness and improved communication—our vision and mission here at Ivy Sea. Mission can inform what we do, such as the products we offer, or it can be about how we work and interact with others in the course of our business. If the vision is a grand ideal, the mission is one or several of the many practical paths that might help shepherd that ideal into reality.

"Mission comes to us; we don't go to it. Mission bangs us over the head and expects us to respond."

Rev. Stuart Hoke,
St. Paul's Chapel,
New York

Core Values. *Values* is another word that's been worn out by mindless and insincere use, but that doesn't make the need to know and articulate your values any less important. Core values or principles might be likened to the spine of your business (or whatever other effort you might undertake), the tenets that allow you to begin realizing your mission and vision in the world, starting with your behavior in your own shop. As an organization grows larger and requires layers of hierarchy and process to keep all of the disparate parts aligned with operating goals, a statement of core values becomes more of a suggested way of operating, an optional guide, for individuals within the group.

"Good, the more communicated, more abundant grows."

JOHN MILTON

What's more, as communication becomes more formal and systematized, it by necessity becomes more oriented to departments or divisions rather than to individuals. In a small enterprise, communication can be less formal and more personal; in a big-vision small business, practices of right relationship forge the link even more directly and effectively between the organization's shared values and an individual's personal core values. The smaller and more autonomous the group—whether a small business, nonprofit, or group within a larger organization—the more true it is that "work is personal."

In a big-vision small business, your clearly defined core values, mission, and vision unite to form the lens through which you will view every decision you make during the course of the quarter or year, and by which you measure your effectiveness in and progress toward manifesting your big-vision operating tenets in the daily activities of your enterprise. What if you haven't articulated your vision, mission, or core values? It's never too late to begin right where you are.

Why Do You Have to Reflect upon and Articulate Your Vision?

Reflecting upon and articulating your vision, mission, and core values is important to help you and, if applicable, your partners and employees, get very clear on exactly what it is you're doing and exactly why you're choosing to spend most of your waking hours doing it. With a vision that stems from your very core, you'll be able to answer the questions that surface, often more than once, for all business owners: "Why am I doing this? What in the world was I thinking?"

In addition, the fruits of your visioning process give you the raw material for a firmly rooted action plan and allow you to make decisions throughout the year as to whether various opportunities or responses are aligned. Capturing your vision—and your plan, for that matter—on paper takes time, reflection, and work, but it's a touchstone you can see, feel, and read aloud when pressures grow and the mission seems murky.

A Reflection on Where We Spend Our Time and Energy

Why are you expanding your business, adding employees, diversifying your products or services, moving from your home office to outside space or from a small space to a larger one? Because you can? Because you should? Bad answers. Since you're going to be the one giving up precious time and energy that could be spent with family, friends, or a favored client project or charitable effort, you have to know that the business is worth as much or more than those other things. You might say, "Well, I want to build the business and maybe sell it so we have something to retire on." Well, what if you died next year? What if you had an eternity? Would you still have made the right decision on how to best spend your time? Would the sole focus on pursuing one model of numerical business growth still have been worthwhile? Is the traditional model of numerical growth the only path to your retirement vision? What makes you think it holds less risk than any other path?

Such questions can be applied to many of the issues and decisions we make along the path of creating and sustaining our business. And when we know what our vision is at any given time, these questions become easier to answer. Our vision for our business guides us. If you haven't articulated your vision or haven't reevaluated it annually at least, you're hiking tough terrain without a guide. With it, you'll have an important source of inspiration for you and your team.

The following chapter features a profile that offers a "fly on the wall" perspective of how vision—the sense of doing something wonderful in the world—can guide a big-vision small-business owner through the peaks and val-leys, hurdles and leaps of operating his enterprise in the real world. The re-maining chapters of this section offer a closer look at visioning practices to help clarify and articulate your vision, as well as practices and exercises to help you leverage the power of big-vision small business by linking your vision and core values to the work that takes place within your organization each day.

Chapter 9

VISION PROFILE: THE CAT DOCTOR

KATH'REN BAY AND ALEXIS Higdon co-founded The Cat Doctor in Boise, Idaho, to provide veterinary care in a welcoming, comfortable environment for felines and their humans. But the road to their big-vision small-business dream was rocky, making the clarity and strength of their founding vision a crucially important beacon for their journey.

Higdon had worked in veterinary clinics from the age of seventeen, doing everything from cleaning kennels to operating the front desk. While in her thirties, she became a veterinary technician and at age 45 completed her doctorate in veterinary medicine. She and Bay envisioned creating the ultimate in health and hospitality for cats by incorporating several of the 12 big-vision priorities into the operation of the clinic they would launch.

"We wanted a place that looked like you were going to Grandma's house, and in working only with cats you can have casual antique furniture and area rugs with hardwood floors," says Bay. With very specific business and lifestyle priorities in mind, the two scoured demographic information on the city's neighborhoods to find one area that suited their needs. Then, after a two-year search for the perfect location, Higdon and Bay bought a 50-year-old Boise farmhouse and established Idaho's first cats-only old-fashioned veterinary hospital and hotel. Compared to the challenges that would follow in the coming year, finding the right city and location in which to manifest their vision would seem easy.

"The period between June 1996 and the time we actually opened in May 1997 was a financial nightmare," remembers Bay. Higdon continued working in a Seattle veterinary hospital and Bay stayed with friends in Boise while they worked out the financial complexities and started plans to renovate the farmhouse into a hospital. Despite having a thoroughly researched business proposal and impeccable credentials, Higdon and Bay were denied financing by one bank after another—eight banks in all.

"Nothing is more likely to help a person overcome or endure troubles than the consciousness of having a task in life."

VICTOR FRANKL

"We suspect that there may have been some discrimination with us as a couple or because we were women and older, but mostly they just didn't understand what we were trying to do. They weren't familiar with the concept of a feline-only veterinary hospital, although they are common elsewhere in the United States," says Bay. Fortunately, the owner of the property was willing to work with the partners, allowing time to secure the necessary loans. At the ninth and last bank in Boise, they found someone willing to take the risk to help finance their big-vision small business. "The banking representative was a woman and a cat owner who got our vision and really fought for us," says Bay. "We got our SBA loan in January, but by then the city building codes had changed, pushing our construction costs 36 percent higher. We had to lease all our startup equipment and supplies. When we opened our doors, we had 10 dollars in the bank."

But financing wasn't the last hurdle the partners had to leap. "We hadn't been opened three days when our autoclave in surgery caught fire. It filled the hospital with smoke and we had to call every friend and family member to bring fans to clear the air. Not more than an hour after the fire was handled, we had a flood and ended up with suds in the hall. Then a client came running out of the bathroom—the toilet had overflowed. Toward the end of the day, I was trying to do the closing and the computer crashed! Alexis and I got up, walked out the door, and walked down the street. And I said, 'If this is what it's going to be like, I don't think I can handle it.' But we just kept that vision in front of us, and now we laugh about it!" says Bay.

Despite these challenges, the two kept faith in their dream. "We wanted to provide a special type of service and create the means to do that," says Higdon. Intent on having an environment that was more pleasant than the typical clinic, Bay and Higdon made sure their facility had ample windows for natural lighting. They selected soothing pastel colors, installed natural-spectrum lighting, and placed wicker furniture on the front porch. And they're equally adamant about fostering right relationships with employees and clients.

"Because we've been employees, we know what's needed to feel valued and instructed well. We're committed to our staff, and they're committed to us," says Bay. The partners therefore offer excellent wages, full health benefits, disability and retirement programs, reasonable work hours, and a supportive, familylike work environment—perks not always associated with small enterprises or veterinary clinics, which are often run on shoestring budgets. Because of such policies, the vision for the clinic is one that employees are proud to be associated with. This is the case in many big-vision small businesses that see higher morale and a sense of meaning as results of an inspiring vision and aligned action.

"Their sense of pride and ownership is incredible," says Bay. "The feedback we get is that they're proud to work in an excellent hospital where people really care. It's sad to say, but in businesses throughout the country you have a great variance in commitment to the client. Our employees have a sense of inner satisfaction in being associated with a business like this. We don't have gossip or pettiness, and we as owners set the example."

Higdon, Bay, and The Cat Doctor's staff work to follow through on their commitment to their clients. "We have a great facility, on a corner lot with trees and flower beds. The parking lot and yard are well tended and immaculate, and we've had clients say that if we keep the place this clean, they know we're taking good care of their cats," says Bay. The investments in the facilities aren't the only factors that help distinguish The Cat Doctor from a more average enterprise that might view such expenditures as an unnecessary drain on potential profits. The pace and personal connection between patients and clinic staff are also high priorities for qualitative excellence.

"Our three doctors are pleasant and approachable, and we schedule 30 minutes per appointment in contrast to the industry norm of 15 or 20 minutes. We have personal business cards for every employee, and there isn't a client who walks in the door that doesn't get a follow-up telephone call from a doctor or technician." The group's genuine care for clients manifests in other ways as well. In addition to a friendly welcome, first-time feline clients receive a home-made catnip toy. The clinic also features coloring books for visiting children and, at the other end of the thoughtfulness spectrum, offers invoices and individual care packets that are carefully designed to be legible and clear.

"As time goes on, our vision is the same, the philosophy is the same," says Bay. "We're more flexible now. We don't panic any more when something comes up and we need to do something differently. Even though we work hard and make personal sacrifices, we feel incredibly blessed to do the work we love and be with people we care about, so we feel we're always on the receiving end."

And Bay's advice to other big-vision, small-business owners who strive for something beyond just quantitative accomplishment to offer something extraordinary? "Keep the vision at all times, and then hang onto your hat, because you've got the tiger by the tail!"

Taking the Vision into Action

This profile, along with the stories included in the previous section on growth, give some sense of how a clear and inspiring vision can be an important anchor and guide during times of challenge and transformation. They help to demonstrate the ways in which your vision of what's possible gives you a place to land in the midst of chaos; some baseline measure from which you can recommit and plot the way to transformation. As Carolina PetSpace owner Ellen Kruskie says, most big-vision small-business owners have invested so much—personally and financially—that persevering in the face of challenge or crisis is the only option they recognize. Why? The vision of making a more qualitative contribution, one that goes beyond owning a store and selling products to meet revenue goals, is so compelling that it helps them withstand the inevitable cycles that are a part of any journey. And since the risks are their own and they tend to be the sole or primary investor, big-vision small-business owners can more readily decide to pursue idealistic as well as financial goals and opt to wait patiently for a longer-term return.

These stories also suggest that an effective big small-business vision, inspiring though it might be, must be linked with the daily decisions and actions of those in the organization. What helps to connect the two? A good plan. The next chapter takes a look at the planning process as it relates to big-vision small-business stewardship, and then moves into discussions about practical approaches.

Chapter 10

To Plan or Not to Plan

WHO HAS TIME for planning when you're so busy working? A good plan can be a pathway that offers guidance on how you might align the everyday work of your organization with your vision. It helps you identify how organizational behavior is influenced by the vision and guiding values. You could say that a plan is your vision's more tactical road to reality. The problem? Most conventional plans seem a world apart from vision, values, passions, or principles, except perhaps for two: growing bigger and getting wealthier.

Most traditional plans are so rational, so detached in their quantitative focus, that they don't connect with the organization's people or behaviors at all. Despite the disconnect in most conventional strategic plan formats, there is great value in adopting some manner of formalized visioning and planning process. If a big-vision small-business owner wants to manifest her vision authentically and effectively, she must find a way to create or adapt a planning process that better suits the more organic, visionary nature of her way of being in business.

In our work at Ivy Sea, both within our organization and with our clients, we create tailored visioning and planning processes that are appropriate to the circumstances, time frame, and individuals involved. Our processes almost always end with a direct connection to the plan, complete with action steps and timetables that participants have articulated and assigned. Such is the way of the big-vision small-business owner. How is this different from the norm, and what approaches are optimal for vision-driven small enterprises?

Many an expert, book, and journal highlight the importance of having a business plan, and there's no shortage of information regarding how to do one, so most people would assume that business planning is a no-brainer and that all business leaders do strategic plans. Departments of large corporations are required by senior executives to produce strategic plans and budgets for at least two reasons: to allow those in the company's highest echelons to approve the plans, and to provide some accountability regarding how investors' money will be spent and what types of returns investors might expect. This requirement is reasonable, particularly in a large enterprise where many divisions and departments are responsible for producing the product and making good on promises to investors.

That's not the case in most small businesses, where the decision maker, risk taker, and investor are one and the same. Compared to a larger enterprise, the small business is a microcosm and thus requires much less formal or stringent processes, including planning. Many small-business owners—like most individuals—don't have a formal, written plan at all, for reasons previously mentioned. In having so many roles and having direct access to everyone in the enterprise, including customers, it's just easier to operate organically, with the vision and strategy stored in the business owner's brain. Since the cause-effect time frames are much shorter in small enterprises, maintaining some degree of flexibility or adaptability is indeed very wise.

Also, because the vast majority of small-enterprise owners don't have access to conventional business loans, or don't choose to expend the energy needed to cut through the red tape for an SBA loan, a traditional business plan isn't needed. Even in cases in which business owners create a plan as a requirement for getting bank financing, the plans often collect dust or are relegated to the deep recesses of a file drawer, never to be seen—much less reviewed—again. It's not until a crisis, the need for formal financing or chaos brought about by a growth spurt, that these owners opt for some sort of more formalized planning process.

While the myriad reasons that small-business owners might avoid planning are understandable, there are many benefits to committing a vision and plan to paper, including those related to prominent issues that arise at some point for most business owners: finding the right life-work balance, deciding whether and how to grow, staying clear and motivated in the business, breaking free of crisis-to-crisis management, deciding when or whether to take or turn away business, and finding and maintaining good relationships with employees, clients, and suppliers. A big-vision small-business owner knows that, as with reflecting on and clarifying the guiding vision, finding an appropriate planning approach and making time for it are a key priority. Big visions rarely manifest themselves into reality by accident or complacency, and big-vision small enterprises are anything but complacent or mediocre.

According to Deborah Danielson, president of Danielson Financial Group in Las Vegas, Nevada, a solid business plan can help big-vision small-business owners avoid—or at least more easily navigate—some of the more painful business realities. "Business owners really do need a business plan," says Danielson, who does plans for her own business as well as advising others. "I've talked with clients who might say, 'I have this great idea,' but without a plan they're just buying themselves a job.

"The reality is that getting the business going will take at least double the money and double the time a business owner might think," she says. "It takes a long time to establish word-of-mouth recognition, and people need to have the money to see that through. Or they'll tell me, 'I didn't think it would be this hard.' It will be; it might get much easier and you might make more money in the long run, but for most people, you've got to do the work up front." Danielson is a business-planning evangelist because, for her, a business plan helps an owner anticipate and prepare for the inevitable challenges.

San Antonio–based Jim Matson of Matson Multimedia agrees. "People make the mistake of not asking the hard questions when they start their business," says Matson, who saw this when many people fell prey to the mass downsizings that occurred in the 1980s. "Because they had money from severance packages and didn't need to get bank financing, no one asked the tough questions that a bank would have asked." As a result, says Matson, many of these new business owners never prepared a business plan and didn't scrutinize their concept or the market, including the multimedia field Matson is in, and ended up with failed businesses as a result. "Some people bought expensive equipment but never researched the market and who else, including me, was providing the same service," he says. "They ended up owning the equipment but no business."

So Why Don't Business Owners Plan?

Let's face it: business owners can be a prickly, individualistic lot. Many people opt for ownership of a small business rather than employment because they like not having to carry out someone else's dictates, particularly when the direction seems off and too much time seems spent in meetings and on organizational navel gazing. They don't particularly like people telling them what to do, and they start their own shop because they think they can do it better. So it's no wonder that most ignore the outside dictum for elaborate business planning. They just want to get to work improving the world and the way things are done. Who has time for bureaucratic bungling when they're on a mission or just enjoying the everyday lifestyle and challenges of being a small-business owner?

Many of the big-vision small-business owners with whom I spoke cited just these causes for balking on the formal strategic planning process: the belief that detailed planning blocks opportunity, creativity, and an intuitive approach to managing the business; the inability to find the time, due to the vast demands of business ownership; and the perception that the planning process seems too cumbersome and overwhelming. To find our way to approaches that work for big-vision small businesses, we have to delve a bit deeper into the beliefs around conventional planning processes.

Belief No. 1: Planning Blocks Opportunity, Creativity, and Intuition

Many business owners like the freedom and challenge of running their business organically and view a formal planning process as a waste of time that could be better spent getting and serving customers or developing new ideas for products and services. Plus, for qualitative entrepreneurs—whose small businesses are a vehicle for learning, excellence, experimentation, service, and quality of life—flexibility is both appealing and necessary for the experience they want to create. For these individuals, too much planning is worse than no planning at all.

"Business planning can be done prematurely," says Al Lovata, chief executive officer of Boston-based Be Our Guest, Inc. Lovata joined the company as its fourth employee and now presides over the 70-plus employee organization. "As long as you know there's a need for your product or service and you know you've got it priced correctly, a lot of the other information can get in the way." Lovata has seen the need for formalized planning increase as the organization expanded. "When you're smaller, if you want to change direction, it's easier," he says. "You do something, see what happens. If you're right, great; if not, you learn from it and take the learning forward. When you're a bigger organization, you've got to do more formal planning. How you respond to challenges and change the company accordingly becomes more complex, because you've got a larger group of people with different levels of understanding and responsibility."

Brian Rogers of Information Insights in Fairbanks, Alaska, agrees that planning can be organic or more formal, depending on the company's needs at any given time. "We've been opportunistic, having an idea of what our competencies are and letting opportunities take us in a new direction," says Rogers. "In a consulting firm, where the assets are intellectual, there's a certain amount of intellectual chaos required, and we take advantage of opportunities that come along and aren't going to let a plan get in the way of that creativity."

Rogers says his group preferred keeping a capability summary—a synopsis of the talents, skills, assets, resources, and time available within the group to serve client needs—rather than a more conventional business plan that includes an executive summary, an introduction, a historical overview, a market summary, a competitive analysis, and the various other intellectual and seemingly far removed aspects of such a plan format. "Our approach has been to have a good handle at all times on the capacity of the company to do work versus the amount of work there is to be done, and managing that so you're not pushing everyone to 100 percent of their capacity," he says. "There's always enough work to keep people busy, but if a new opportunity came in, we would be able to balance things to accommodate it." While Rogers's approach worked from the organization's inception to the recent past, he and his partner prepared a more formalized plan to attract venture capital for several projects now in the pipeline.

Barb Banonis of LifeQuest International in Charleston, West Virginia, prefers not to do traditional business planning because of the constantly changing nature of the market. "My best planning strategy is to know myself and what I have to offer," she says of her personal-development consulting business. "I'm more able to move flexibly into new roles and markets. It can be difficult because people sometimes don't know how to classify you, but it's an asset because they don't classify you."

For Cec Stanford of Prairie Herb Company, planning is a matter of following her intuition and always having a goal. Stanford's company, with five or so part-time employees working from her ranch in Gillette, Wyoming, makes bottled oils and vinegars that are designed to be as beautiful as they are deliciously functional. Prairie Herb products were included in the 1995 *America's Best Foods* book and have received other honors and attention, finding their way to some very famous tables.

"If I have a feeling about a product that we're offering, or if I have a feeling that a change needs to be made, I try to follow my intuition," she says. Stanford says that, for her, it's a different form of business planning—always knowing what your goals are and incorporating your intuition and day-to-day feedback from customers—that works, whether it's accepted by the more traditional business community or not. Even while rejecting formal plans, Stanford has tapped into an advantage that a big-vision small-business owner has: the ability to quickly adapt and act on intuition when an opportunity or issue arises, instead of wasting precious time having to route the idea up through layers of hierarchy or through the morass of organizational politics. "I've taken classes on business planning and had a difficult time finishing the plan because I was running a business at the same time," she says. "Most of the people who finished the perfect business plan never started a business! I just don't have the time." And that leads to a second predominant belief about planning.

Belief No. 2: Business Owners Are Too Busy to Plan

Like Stanford, many small-business owners don't engage in business planning because they find themselves busier than they ever thought possible, with the demands of running the business taking precedence over what they perceive as a long, drawn-out, and not ultimately beneficial planning process. In most small businesses, minimal staffing means that each individual manages several areas of responsibility, and few businesses have the resources to employ a highly paid strategist to spend weeks or months producing a plan. Instead, they go right to the heart of it, using only the information that tells them what they need to know at the time.

"Our planning processes were very informal," says Jackie Fellers, who stepped in to run Fellers Specialty Advertising in San Antonio, Texas, when her husband passed away. "We were just so busy, putting a hundred percent into the business, and growth just came. I never had a need for a business plan." Yet Fellers always made time to review her profit and loss statements on a regular basis, so she knew exactly where the business was from a financial standpoint. "As long as our numbers looked good, that's what I focused on," she says. "You don't want to ignore where you stand financially, because you could wake up one day and be in big trouble."

Kevin Owens, founder of Select Design, Ltd., in Burlington, Vermont, didn't do formal planning but did keep a keen eye on his vision of creating a great place to work and trying to be the best at what Select Design does, an approach he continued to use even when the business grew to more than 50 employees. "Our planning was haphazard," says Owens, "and it seemed as if many decisions got made for us, where things would just happen and opportunities came to us. Our primary focus has been on caring deeply about our clients and their needs." Although Owens's group was more effective at responding to challenges and opportunities as they came up, rather than doing proactive planning, they also expected that to change when the company expanded. "The organization is bigger, the iceberg is bigger, and there's more to lose, quite frankly," he says. "The worst-case scenario is not just about two people failing in a business and feeling crushed. There are a lot more people affected by the failure and success of the business now."

Owens's company grew—in longevity as well as size—thanks to a clear vision and good work, yet the growth has created challenges in addition to the added sense of responsibility for ensuring the company's viability. Despite a larger payroll, he and his partner found themselves busier than ever and still responsible for the lion's share of revenue generation, as well as the firm's operations and financial management. At the time we spoke, Owens was look-ing at how to create more balance between his business and family life and to delegate additional responsibility to others in the business.

These are the very challenges that, regardless of the business's size or one's decision to opt for qualitative evolution or quantitative growth, can be eased somewhat by doing more formal visioning and planning earlier in the life of your business, or by starting wherever you are at the moment. It's no wonder that it doesn't seem feasible, given the perception that business planning has to be an all-or-nothing affair resulting in a four-inch-thick document that took months to prepare and includes details that seem irrelevant to the realities of running a very small business—particularly one driven by vision, mission, val-ues, and other qualitative priorities. But as several of these business owners have indicated, there are options that can be linked together like puzzle pieces to create a workable strategy that helps maintain financial viability while doing the enterprise's more passionate work. A big-vision small-business owner is al-ways looking for ways to marry the two.

While he doesn't commit his vision to paper, Rich Maggiani, another Burlington small-business owner, uses a cash flow–tracking spreadsheet and creative questioning as his planning tool. With bachelor's and master's degrees in business and accounting, Maggiani fully understands the financial aspect of running his marketing and graphic design shop, Page Designs, but doesn't go all out for a traditional planning process. "Looking at numbers on a spread-sheet isn't going to tell you how to be more profitable," says Maggiani. "So tweaking the numbers isn't coming at it from the most productive direction." A spreadsheet also won't tell you what types of employees you need or how to manage them well—an area for which Maggiani's 14-person firm has received statewide recognition. Instead, Maggiani says he asks questions.

Rather than saying "Our costs are too high so let's cut them," Maggiani asks questions such as "Why aren't our sales higher? Why isn't this client relying on us more? Are our expenses too high?" "I've learned to look at the bigger goal," he says, "asking 'This is what we're trying to get at here; is our approach work-ing? Is it linked to one of our highest goals?'" Maggiani's approach relies on the fact that he always knows what his highest goals are, which include creating livable jobs that add to an individual's life, ensuring an environment of respect and trust, and reinvesting profits in the company.

For Pat Heffernan, copresident of Marketing Partners, Inc., another Burlington firm, taking the time for visioning at startup has provided a solid foundation as the business has evolved and grown. Heffernan, whose company has about 12 people, including the two partners, worked with her business partner on a very detailed vision of what they wanted the business to become. "We did everything from envision what it would be like for our clients walking into our ideal office, to how our employees would be ideally treated, to what we envisioned 10 years into the business," says Heffernan.

But Heffernan and her partner didn't opt for creating a traditional business plan either, despite her own preference for formal planning and a master's degree in business administration. "We had our mission, our values, some key words, and thoughts about where we wanted to be," she says, "and we made an investment in talking about some scenarios, how we would handle specific things." The two partners do a planning retreat once a year, where they look at how they're doing, whether the business is on track with established goals, and where they want to be.

The planning process can also shed light on what's possible for a big-vision small business and its owners, something Keith Rollins of Portland, Maine, emphasizes. "Whether you're looking for financing or you're just trying to focus your thoughts, a business plan is important," says Rollins, who helped establish The Resource Hub. "A business plan doesn't have to be stagnant; it can be always evolving, changing on a weekly or even a daily basis. But it helps you focus on what you want to achieve, and it helps you gauge how well you're doing."

"If you're not meeting projections," says Rollins, "you can consider what changes you need to make in the business. Many business owners underestimate their opportunities, or the business underperforms because they don't want to do a plan."

As Owens, Maggiani, Heffernan, and Rollins demonstrate, visioning and planning, like the business itself, can be flexible, creative, energizing, and clarifying. There are options that lie between doing the conventional plan and winging it. The trick is to adopt visioning and planning processes that, while tailored to your personality and time-management reality, are designed to collect key information from your mind and capture it on paper so it can be reviewed more objectively for gaps and shared effectively with the people on your team so the plan translates into action.

Chapter 11

APPROACHES TO VISIONING AND PLANNING

OVER THE YEARS, I've come to prefer specific types of visioning or planning processes that are dynamic and appropriate for smaller vision-driven organizations, whether they're just starting up or needing transformation or an inspiration boost. As a result, I've refined a "vision-to-action" model that I've found helpful in yielding a creative, energizing visioning experience as well as a more practical bridge to planning and action.

Most other visioning and planning approaches I've seen too often segregate visioning from planning, with the only link being the appearance of a vision and mission statement at the beginning of a more detailed quantitative plan. Many also lack a mixture of appropriate visual, kinesthetic, and auditory exercises that help make the experience more creative and motivating. Such approaches may be applicable to certain situations or organizations, but they weren't appropriate for ours, Ivy Sea, Inc., nor were they for many of the groups with whom we've worked to identify that core of vision and clarity from which all planning should spring.

Because each organization is unique at any given time, depending on the owner's vision and the organization's stage of evolution, a visioning approach needs to be tailored to the organization. The staples of a worthwhile process include reflection, dialogue, brainstorming, assessment, and bridging and can pretty easily be made part of the organization's discussion and implementation norms. Big-vision small businesses want to generate the energy from the vision, passion, and talent within the group that will take their shared vision into the world. Let's take a closer look at the building blocks that can lead you deeper into clear vision and from there into big-vision small-business action.

REFLECTION

Western culture in particular encourages action over reflection, yet the most informed decision making, particularly in a big-vision small business with strong participation by its founder, is that which includes a balance between what St. Teresa of Avila called the *activa* and the *contemplativa*. To rise above mediocrity and capitalize on the strengths of small scale, the big-vision small business relies on both.

Visioning programs that don't include time for personal reflection, for connecting with sources of inspiration and intuition, and that don't integrate organizational and individual vision work risk failure by ignoring the strong link between personal motivation and organizational outcomes. Numerous surveys underscore the effect of individual attitudes on such organizational success factors as sales, productivity, and morale. By incorporating reflection exercises into a visioning program, participants have time to identify their own attitudes and motivations and create the space in which intuitive insights and personal connections to the organization's vision, mission, and values might arise. For a visioning program, reflection components might include time for contemplation, nature walks, sitting with thought-provoking questions, journaling, or one-on-one conversations between the facilitator and participant followed by time alone.

DIALOGUE

Dialogue might be defined as a conversation or exchange of ideas between two or more people. Surely anyone who works with others knows that dialogue is an essential part of our daily drama, whether at home, at the office, or in the community. What's more, we know that the more effective our dialogue, the more effective and rewarding are our days, including any work we do on personal and organizational visioning.

Most people assume they know what dialogue is: the opposite of a monologue, where one does all the talking. Unfortunately, most individuals don't listen very well, so even in what seems to them to be a dialogue, they do a lot of talking and very little listening. Thus we suggest Dialogue, a more formal communication process that is employed to work through misunderstandings, enhance understanding and community, engage more effective listening, and reveal new (and healthier) ways of working. Dialogue stems from the wisdom of many cultures and a variety of practitioners, including physicist David Bohm. Working from the observations of anthropologists working with indigenous cultures, Bohm identified a process by which conversation happens, assumptions and judgments are exposed, perceptual filters are revealed, real listening occurs, and true communication is finally able to emerge.[10]

Dialogue is a particularly appropriate tool at the beginning of a visioning program, when it's important to unearth personal motivations, attitudes, barriers, and perceptions. Dialogue can also be a wonderful way for the group to reflect upon and share perceptions regarding organizational strengths, defining moments, and opportunities for refinement—information that can be taken into brainstorming sessions, assessments, and vision-to-action plans.

BRAINSTORMING

Nobel prize winner Linus Pauling allegedly said, "The best way to have a good idea is to have lots of ideas." The purpose of a brainstorm session is to generate a whole roster of ideas and possibilities from which to choose. Like Dialogue, a skillfully facilitated brainstorm session differs greatly from the impromptu, garden-variety sessions common in many workplaces. In a more carefully planned brainstorm session, the facilitators can craft an agenda varied enough to get the creativity flowing (or brains storming). They'll also moderate the discussion in a way that engages everyone—not just the more dominant, extroverted participants—and culls information that might not be visible in a more low-key discussion. There are a variety of exercises and facilitative tools for effective brainstorming, and any agenda should be tailored to the needs and personalities of particular groups, as well as the different ways of learning and digesting information. Brainstorming is appropriate when you want to open the discussion to generate ideas and unearth potentialities.

Assessment

It's surprising how often in my own client work I ask someone, after listening to him wonder what someone else might think or whether an assumption is correct, "Have you asked *them*?" the answer is "No." A big-vision small-business relies upon input from stakeholders in order to identify opportunities for refinement and continued progress in the rise above mediocrity.

For a rich visioning program, gather perspectives from key constituencies so you can assess what perceptions, attitudes, and motivations those individuals or groups really have regarding your organization. Assessments can be formal or informal—surveys, interviews, or conversational pulse checks. You can gather input yourself with members of your group or hire a third party to gather information for you. Regardless of the method you choose, get feedback so your visioning rests on a real, solid foundation versus a flimsy, assumption-based house of cards.

"It is not good enough for things to be planned—they still have to be done; for the intention to become a reality, energy has to be launched into operation."

Pir Vilayat Khan

Why is it important to include such an assessment with visioning? Because some of your visioning work addresses how you'd like the organization to be experienced and perceived by others, such as customers or employees, including a comparison of any gaps between current reality and the envisioned scenario. Feedback can be tapped prior to the visioning program as well as during the visioning program to test specific options you might be considering or to create understanding or invite participation of key groups who weren't represented in the initial stages.

Bridging

Even the most wonderful vision isn't worth much if there's no bridge between it and your business's day-to-day activities. And fusing an organization's action with an inspiring vision and sense of mission is what helps to distinguish big-vision small-businesses from other enterprises.

Many visioning approaches don't bridge effectively enough so that the resulting actions of the organization are tempered by the vision. In that case, the visioning process is just an exercise, albeit perhaps an enjoyable one, and the vision is little more than a bunch of nice-sounding words on the company brochure, employee handbook, and Web site.

In our own work at Ivy Sea and in our work with clients we have always emphasized the importance of ending visioning sessions with an action plan. In our bridging portion of the visioning work, the more creative, inspirational content gets chiseled down into a selection of operational examples or action items that help to make sure that the visioning work won't end when the visioning program wraps. While the program may not yield a detailed strategic plan, it should yield an action list that speaks to how the vision can be translated into the organization's daily activities, starting immediately. Bridging exercises are tailored to begin narrowing the discussion, organizing options and priorities, and capturing the information into some actionable format, like a chart or matrix.

Follow-Up

At the end of your visioning session, make sure your action plan includes check points scheduled during the subsequent months to assess which action items have been completed, which have been modified, and what vision-supportive activities are high priorities for the coming quarter. Neglect follow-up, and you increase the likelihood that all of the wonderful energy and terrific opportunities generated during your visioning session will fizzle and fall flat. Creating a vision and integrating that vision into the daily operations of the business is an organic, not a static, process.

Consider the vision a garden, with the visioning process serving as the space-clearing, garden-designing, and soil-tilling phase. The action plan and subsequent status check-ins comprise the planting, watering, fertilizing, and weeding that the garden requires if it is to support an eventual harvest. In other words, the follow-up phase is where the heart and soul of gardening takes place and, as gardeners know, often produces much joy and satisfaction in and of itself. If the tools used and the products produced from your visioning program are specific and actionable, they'll provide all the reference material you need for the first check-in session. After that, you can incorporate vision follow-up activities into your organizational communications, from your staff meetings to your project plans, and into your annual retreats and celebrations.

These vision building blocks form the foundation of an effective visioning process and expand the process and the vision itself—so that it has a life beyond the visioning sessions. For many organizations or teams, the visioning process is simply an activity to be completed, yielding a statement that appears in subsequent documents referring to the business or project; once the statement is crafted, the participants assume the visioning work is done. It's not. The visioning process is a beginning, and while the visioning processes we at Ivy Sea have refined take this into account and include check-in points throughout the year, the responsibility remains with the big-vision small-business owner and her company to safeguard and shepherd the vision they've created and look for practical ways that their vision can be manifested in action.

Exercise: Putting It All Together

The following questions, which are among the resources we share on Ivy Sea Online, may serve as good reflection-and-dialogue starters for you and your group.[11] These discussion points guide you through your present scenario, fears, strengths, and possibilities and help you unearth and make the most of your big-vision assets and opportunities.

- *Take stock of your situation.* There is nothing to fear but fear itself, as Franklin Delano Roosevelt said. Grab a notepad, flipchart, or whiteboard, pens, and several of your colleagues, if appropriate, and do a thorough check-in on circumstances, resources, and possibilities. Free-floating anxiety or a lack of clarity are dangerous because you can't work well from those states for an extended period of time. By untangling the current state of affairs (in this case, regarding your business or livelihood) and reacquainting yourself with the points around which you can gain clarity, you can better know what you're working with and take action. Use the following list to guide your vision-to-action check-in.
- *Assess your strengths.* Taking inspiration from approaches such as "appreciative inquiry,"[12] identify all of the things that work well in

and for your enterprise. For example, your previous experience in creating opportunities and overcoming challenges or anxiety-provoking circumstances is a strength. Other strengths may be revealed by positive things others have said about you, reasons people have enjoyed working with you, or even those things that you love to do even if you do them for free or as "value added" in your work. For this part of the exercise, you'll want to unabashedly accentuate the positive and sing your own or your group's praises.

· *Articulate your worst-case scenarios or fears.* Perhaps you fear that the economy won't recover or that a new strategic direction may risk your organization's survival. Maybe you fear that you'll lose your financial standing or the material assets upon which you base your perceptions of success. Or you may fear that you'll go bankrupt, that your traditional customer base will no longer support your business, that you'll have to reduce your payroll and lay off valued employees, or that you'll no longer enjoy or feel challenged by your work. These scenarios may shake your confidence, give you an upset stomach, or have you waking in the middle of the night with anxious thoughts of failure. As frightful as these scenarios can be, we often overestimate them, or at least underestimate our ability to deal with them despite their unpleasantness. One of the best ways to decrease our fears of the ghosts in the closet is to open the closet door and turn on the light. This exercise can be done proactively as well as when you're in the midst of a specific period of challenging circumstances.

· *List assets and contingencies.* Now that you've unmasked your worst-case scenarios, make a list of anything you consider to be one of your assets or resources. Include everyone and everything rather than simply limiting your list to professional, financial, and material assets. What might you still have or do if faced with these worst-case options? When in the past do you remember overcoming difficult circumstances and prevailing in the face of challenges that might have seemed insurmountable at the time? On whom could you count for assistance or support if you were to face any one of the things on your "fearsome scenarios" list? What stories, whether from your own family tree or more general history, bolster your sense of grit and resourcefulness? What and whom matters more to you than professional status and financial or material assets? These are all good things to include on your assets roster.

- *Note where you can be of service.* Mother Theresa offered very practical advice when she said, "If you want to know how to change the world, pick up a broom." Some wisdom traditions emphasize that "you find yourself when you lose yourself" in service to others, but you don't have to practice any particular wisdom tradition to know that being of service to others feels good and takes your focus off of your own shortcomings. That's a great start. This exercise isn't about what's profitable (though it might come back to you ultimately in that way) nor what charitable contributions you can make, but rather how you might help meet community needs through your organization.

  For example, in the wake of the September 11, 2001, terrorist attacks, local bookstores found themselves to be important information sources and gathering spaces for neighbors in search of information or just comfort. While large-scale tragedies magnify such needs for community and mutual support, the needs—and opportunities for service—always exist. Ask yourself how you or your business can be of greater service or help create a more enriched, positive, supportive community. This list should include and go beyond your current professional product and service offerings.

- *Imagine the possibilities.* Put your cynicism, criticism, and negativity on the shelf for this part of the program. Taking a look over the things you've listed based on the exercises above, imagine how you can reinvigorate or revitalize current products or services. Who else might benefit from the strengths and assets you've listed? Are there potential customers that you just haven't considered before only because flush times didn't require that degree of creative thinking? Are there other ways that you could organize skills, assets, and strengths to create new products or services that fit current and future marketplace needs? Have you acquired new knowledge or experience that could benefit others? What accomplishments would you like to celebrate as you wrap the coming year? Without mentioning your industry, products, or services, what would you like people to be able to say about your contributions to the marketplace, your community, and the world?

- *Brainstorm opportunities.* Having identified assets, resources, areas of service, and a multitude of possibilities, consider what opportunities might exist for bringing those ideals or concepts into your daily, weekly, monthly, and annual activities. What resources and revenues will you need to meet your desired quality of life and sustainability (individual or organizational)? What organizations exist that could benefit from the services or products you provide? How can potential avenues of service be integrated into your way of doing business (or doing your job)? With whom can you create mutually beneficial partnerships to provide your products or services in a way that meets a need while ensuring a fair revenue in return? With whom can you partner and collaborate to identify or pursue opportunities? To whom can you turn for trusted advice and a helpful perspective to put the needed resources into place and create opportunities? How can you apply the four big-vision keys to raise your level of work to master craftsmanship?

· *Align your vision with action.* Continuing your dialogue started in the exercises above, what action can you take today to begin creating resources and opportunities and fulfilling this vision of what's possible? What can you do this week? This month? In the coming quarter? What do your insights and observations from the above exercises mean for how you conduct your business, create and maintain your relationships, market your products or services, and interact within your company?

While you can add other categories and exercises to your list, the ones above offer a place to start as you launch a journey to a new level of excellence and meaning. By reflecting on these questions and engaging your group in dialogue you will have an anchor and resource as you check in each month and quarter to assess your progress, identify new resources and opportunities, or upgrade your goals for the year. For more ideas and dialogue-starter questions, visit our public-service Web site, Ivy Sea Online (www.ivysea.com).

Working from Your Own Standards

In any organizational visioning and planning work, it's important to include the more contemplative activities, not just to create fertile ground for brilliant insights but also to feel confident that the standards you've selected as success measures are your own. All too often, a small-business owner works for years and invests much in the way of time, energy, money, and personal sacrifices to achieve standards that, in hindsight, weren't important to her at all. She had worked according to standards regarded as important by someone else: a parent, a culture, an academic, a management guru, a business journal, a former group of friends or fellow graduates, even her lawyer or accountant. While gathering perspectives from any or all such people is worthwhile, the decision regarding the type of organization you build, its unique way of working, and the nature of its products, services, and goals remains a highly personal one.

One area where big-vision small-enterprise owners often choose to operate from mastery-level standards—and truly shine as a result—is in developing an interpersonal skillfulness for relationships that go beyond "delighting your customer" or "winning the war for talent." The next section offers an in-depth perspective on the concept of right relationship and the practical ways a big-vision enterprise can tap into this power source as an area of excellence and development—all opportunities for qualitative growth.

KEY Nº 3:
RIGHT RELATIONSHIP
IS A BIG-VISION CRAFT

"HE ONLY DOES NOT LIVE

IN VAIN WHO EMPLOYS

HIS WEALTH, HIS THOUGHT,

HIS SPEECH TO ADVANCE

THE GOOD OF OTHERS."

Hindu proverb

Chapter 12

RIGHT RELATIONSHIP AS A PATHWAY
FOR QUALITATIVE GROWTH

A FRIEND AND FELLOW business owner frequently says, only half joking, that her business would be great if it were not for her employees and customers. Given that her business has been successful for a decade and she has both a unique work environment and distinguishing service ethic, not to mention a 100 percent referral and repeat rate, she clearly means no disrespect. What she does mean is that her primary challenges of business ownership arise when her desire to foster good relationships collides with the reality that she, her employees, and customers are human beings who don't always behave perfectly. It's a classic case of aiming for high ideals in an imperfect world of psyches, egos, and bottom lines.

For big-vision small-business owners, relationships are not just a key component of the plan to differentiate their business from competing firms but a centerpiece of the vision and a prime opportunity for qualitative growth. Right relationships—whether with staff members, clients, vendors, or the community—require conscious decision making, skillful communication, and more than a little commitment to service and personal development. Such a level of relationship goes beyond the norms or minimum standards for employee relations or customer service. In addition to increasing the likelihood of enjoyable projects and repeat business or referrals, right relationship can in itself be a practice of one's personal mission in the world of work that leads to organizational and personal mastery, as well as spiritual growth.

What are right relationships, and how might a big-vision small-business owner integrate those standards into the activities of his enterprise? One possible definition comes by way of the fable known as *The Rabbi's Gift:* "As they contemplated in this manner, the old monks began to treat each other with extraordinary respect on the off chance that one among them might be the Messiah. And on the off, off chance that each monk himself might be the Messiah, they began to treat themselves with extraordinary respect." This excerpt appeared in an issue of the Foundation for Community Encouragement's newsletter, *FCE Communiqué.* Following the excerpt, the newsletter editorial staff pondered what this approach might look like in everyday practice:

> *Many of us have heard the story of* The Rabbi's Gift *many times and have been moved by the idea of extraordinary respect expressed in this story. But it would be a shame to leave this vital concept as just a moving story! Here at FCE our goal is to learn and practice how to live out our lives incorporating this principle of extraordinary respect. What does extraordinary respect mean to you? How have you experienced this from others? How do you attempt to live this out in your own life?*[1]

These are excellent questions to ask. Yet we can easily fall into the trap of believing that we're already maintaining right relationships if we attain some degree of success with the business. If we have an acceptable level of referrals and customers and if our employee turnover is low, we might be tempted to think we have no more work to do in relationship building. That might be the case in an average organization but not one aspiring toward alignment with big-vision priorities. To help avoid complacency, we at Ivy Sea test ourselves by asking, "If we ranked our current level of performance in this area at a two, what would a level-ten performance look like?"

A commitment to fostering right relationships includes exploring and putting into action this concept of extraordinary respect, as well as extraordinary thoughtfulness directed at all who come into contact with your business. Extraordinary respect might mean that you don't see your customers simply as walking dollar signs. It might mean viewing employees as human beings instead of "human capital." And both of these perspectives are more likely to be integrated into the practices of a smaller enterprise that is independent from the pressures to maximize returns to major investors.

Extraordinary thoughtfulness, a form of respect in action, might mean that we put ourselves in our customers' shoes, so to speak, so that we know for sure that our interaction leaves them feeling better, not worse, and respected, not de-graded. After dealing with representatives from our business, they should go home to their families feeling full and kind, not de-flated and angry. Right relationship is an ad-mirable and inspiring concept but not an easy one to implement regularly. Such a level of attentiveness requires our presence, our daily effort, and our careful attention.

Extraordinary respect might mean that we don't see our customers simply as walking dollar signs. It might mean viewing employees as human beings instead of "human capital."

One challenge in aspiring toward right relationships is the ability to keep one foot firmly planted in reality; we are, after all, talk-ing about running a business. While such a commitment seems easy from a superficial perspective, particularly given the abundance of customer-service programs and related jargon, it can be frustratingly difficult to find the balance between generosity of spirit and the place where you tolerate disrespectful treatment from others or situations that jeopardize the health of the business. For a big-vision small-business owner, this might manifest in such a strong desire to create a good work environment and happy employees that there isn't enough focus placed on individual responsibility to the organization and its clients. Another symp-tom of imbalance might be keeping wrong-fit employees on staff too long or tolerating an unhealthy or disrespectful client relationship well past the point where it might have been set back on track or ended.

Creating right relationships involves walking a delicate line between offering generous advantages to and ensuring a minimum standard of respectful be-havior from others. And since smaller enterprises are more often associated with a higher degree of experimentation and personal connection, they offer greater latitude—if the owner is game—for being incubators of sorts for different right-relationship practices. In return for a higher commitment to cultivating truly deep relationships, respectful interactions, and positive connections, the big-vision small business can distinguish itself in leaps and bounds from competitors and provide more meaningful, growth-rich opportunities to employees. Where can you start to evaluate your own potential for development in this area? The next chapter introduces seven golden rules for right relationship for your own reflection, dialogue, and skill building.

Chapter 13

GOLDEN RULES FOR RIGHT RELATIONSHIPS

MANY PEOPLE, and many time-honored re-
ligions and life philosophies, have their own unique prescriptions for creating
and sustaining right relationships. One factor that can distinguish big-vision
small enterprises from other organizations is a conscious commitment to setting and reaching a higher standard in relationship. What are the practices that
help these visionary small enterprises to far exceed the norms? There are a few
golden rules that, if honored, can help to provide a foundation for refining the
quality of our interpersonal skillfulness and our relationships with others. The
purpose? To better leverage this opportunity for qualitative growth and develop
an inherent strength of smaller enterprise. Without observing these practices,
it's not possible to have a big-vision small business. We'll explore the ways that
a visionary small enterprise might consider and integrate these concepts later
in the section.

GOLDEN RULE NO. 1: KNOW THYSELF

Paying others extraordinary respect and acting from a place of thoughtfulness
requires that we're not caught up in perpetual stress, frustration, anger, self-
absorption, or ignorance. "Know thyself" isn't an abstraction but rather truly
wise advice. Of course, if it were that easy, everyone would be doing it, and we'd
have a great deal fewer ego collisions in the world. Many people aren't aware of
their own personality masks, or "shadow side," so other people live at the mercy

of their moods. The good news? Life is, or can be, a journey toward increased skillfulness, and the payoff can be gradual rather than delayed. Better yet, since this moment, right now, is all that really exists—the past being behind us and the future not yet real—it's never too late and one is never "too old" to become mindful of the moment or to enrich the quality of our days and our relationships.

The point is not so much to self-obsess or pigeonhole yourself—a common criticism aimed at personality assessments and so-called navel gazing—but to increase our awareness of how we interact in the world and how others might experience us. In learning more about ourselves, we also become more sensitive to and compassionate toward the potential and personality-driven foibles of others. We learn to react less and respond more, and do both more skillfully. We take the time to become more aware so that we increase our opportunities for deeper relationship normally wasted in miscommunicating, misunderstanding, and insisting that we get our way, even in seemingly irrelevant situations.

What can we do to proactively nurture these moments of greater awareness rather than passively settle for accidental brushes with grace? An excellent question for anyone interested in cultivating a big-vision small business. One resource I use in my own awareness-raising practice is the Enneagram, an ancient system of insight that was handed down in the oral tradition of the Sufis—a mystical sect of Islam—and more recently popularized in a number of self-help and organizational psychology books. Though stripped of its deeply spiritual roots in many of today's popular workplace applications, the Enneagram honors the work in progress that is our lives. For me, the Enneagram is more holistic than many popular personality-typing formats, and I keep several books on the subject nearby when I need a wise perspective on an interpersonal challenge. Familiarizing ourselves with the Enneagram and other approaches only increases our level of awareness, highlighting patterns which resonate with us and identify areas of our life's work.

Other disciplines are also important in our attempts to live the examined life, including our religious or spiritual practices—such as prayer, meditation, and communing respectfully with nature and one another. Many people, including many of the big-vision small-business owners with whom I spoke, maintain dedicated practices of reading and talking with others about spiritual and mindset-management topics. Practices for good health, including nutrition and exercise, play an important role, too, in our ability to stay grounded in our center instead of reacting to every hot button (did you ever try to stay grounded when you were rushed, or wired on caffeine and sugar?). This is where life, the journey, offers a wealth of opportunities to practice what we profess to believe—where the difference between saying and doing, believing and being, becomes sometimes painfully evident.

GOLDEN RULE NO. 2: FRAME AND LISTEN

One of the most wonderful concepts used in conflict-resolution programs is deep listening—literally, learning to listen deeply to others with less interference from your ego. That means you train yourself, through practice, to set aside those "But, but, but" and "That's not right" inclinations so you can understand another's point of view. The sad reality is that most people don't listen but rather anxiously await the next opportunity to speak. Most conversations are actually monologues punctuated by periods of waiting to talk. But when someone really listens? Wow. Think about a time when you felt like someone was really listening to you. To be listened to makes us feel valuable, and members of a big-vision small business enjoy making others feel deeply heard and truly valued. That's why deep listening practices provide an excellent opportunity for qualitative growth, right relationship, and increased joy and meaning.[2]

When deep listening is combined with framing, one element of skillful communication, the quality of your interactions can increase dramatically. You've no doubt heard of listening, if not deep listening. But framing? Think about it. What would it be like to build a house without first constructing a frame? It would be a struggle at best, consuming unnecessary resources, and completely impossible at worst, buckling every time you made progress on a certain section.

Communication is the same way. Without the proper framing, we can't be sure our words will stand on their own or be received by others in the way we intend. It doesn't matter if the conversation is electronic, spoken, or written. Without creating context, if we fail to properly state our intentions at the start, chances increase that we'll be misunderstood and others will react to real or imagined slights or threats. You've no doubt experienced those uncomfortable moments, after launching right into some topic or sending out a memo, when you realize that others not only misinterpreted what you said, they've been offended and are angry or upset. And once we begin climbing that emotional ladder, we must spend precious time backtracking, apologizing, and attempting to gain clarity and mutual understanding of our original intention. While these situations can, if we choose to make them so, be rich in learning, they can also be at least sometimes avoided if we approach communication more adeptly.

By first framing the conversation (or taking responsibility for our communication by asking to have the conversation framed), all individuals involved will more likely share the same understanding, thus improving the outcome of our interaction in our daily communications. Here are a few helpful steps to get communication off to a good start:

- *State your intention at the start.* For example, if your intention for a meeting is that the group leave with an increased awareness of a certain issue that they must then translate into an action plan by day's end, say that at the start of the meeting. If your intention for a performance discussion with an employee is that the two of you together identify opportunities to improve the relationship, say so.

- *If you have a specific agenda, say so.* "I'd like to start with this issue, discuss options, then make a decision by the time we're finished meeting. Is this okay with you?"

- *If you're asking for action from others, say so.* "It's important that we get your feedback within 24 hours so the project won't be delayed. The information in this packet is designed to help you provide that feedback as easily as possible."

- *If what you're saying will be controversial or upsetting, say so.* "What I'm going to say may be upsetting for you, and I might not say it as well as I'd hope. But I really need you to hear me out so we can come to the best resolution for each of us."

These steps can help avoid unintentional communication problems that plague most organizations and limit attempts to deepen connections. That such practices are not the norm offers another way to meet big-vision priorities and distinguish the big-vision small business from other businesses. Lest we assume that we have no room for growth in this area, read on for the next golden rule.

GOLDEN RULE NO. 3: BE AWARE OF ASSUMPTIONS, JUDGMENTS, AND FILTERS

What do assumptions, judgments, and filters have to do with fostering right relationship? Almost everything, since they inform how we view and react or respond to people and situations around us. Is it possible to practice extraordinary respect and thoughtfulness from a place of absolute certainty, where we don't even entertain the notion that there exists a perspective other than our own? No. We look around us, process that information through filters we've gained during the course of our upbringing, make assumptions about whether something is right or wrong, and issue a judgment that sets the stage for subsequent action. The less we're aware of when and how we do this, the more likely our chances for miscommunication and less than optimal interactions with others. The smaller the group, the easier it is to foster a shared commitment to interpersonal skillfulness that has a positive effect on the business and all of its shareholders. As with everything else in life, our filters, assumptions, and judgments find their way into the very fabric of our business, which is why big-vision small-business owners encourage refinement in these areas.

For example, how often do business owners create work environments based on their own preferences for what they wanted as an employee? Pretty frequently. This isn't necessarily a bad thing. In fact, it can be directly responsible for the creation of a unique, respectful, quirky, and engaging company culture, which is possible in a small enterprise. But what happens when the owner's decisions are based solely on one or two past experiences, to the point where the effect on the workplace—and company health—is dysfunctional or limiting?

For example, an owner who was previously employed in a structureless and chaotic office might go to the opposite extreme, creating a workplace that is stifling in its devotion to regulation and policy. The person who was bruised by his participation in a closed, bureaucratic office environment might become too fervent about avoiding any structure at all. And our filters and assumptions have other far-reaching effects on our organizational culture and health: we might draw conclusions about an employee's potential or a prospective opportunity that, without awareness of our filters, prove inaccurate and thus limiting. We might make snap judgments and react to a client's feedback, thus missing an opportunity for a deepened connection. By uncovering and acknowledging at least some of our assumptions, we expand the territory in which potential and opportunity like awaiting our awareness. Just one more step forward in our quest for qualitative excellence.

Finding the right balance requires that we become more aware of ourselves and how we run the business and check out our own experience with feedback from employees and regular review of anecdotes from other business owners. We might ultimately make the same choices, but we'll be more confident that those choices are congruent with our priorities for our big-vision small business and thus the work environment we wish to create (and that our customers find preferable).

Golden Rule No. 4: Ensure Common Understanding and Expectations

Many interpersonal low points occur when we assume that others understand us (or we them) but in fact they have no clear idea what we expect or understand what we're looking for. The result? Friction and discord when day-to-day circumstances shine light on mismatched desires and expectations. In the workplace in businesses small and large, this often begins on the very first day of our interactions with prospective employees and continues through the employer-employee relationship until the employee leaves the organization or time and tension help to chisel an acceptable level of agreement (or dysfunction). And the same is true of relationships with clients and vendors, where assumed understanding ends in disputes that often damage trust and jeopardize the relationship. Why do business owners fail to communicate expectations? One reason includes tight timelines and pressures for quantitative return, resulting in a faster pace and less time for thoughtful, deliberate communication and follow-through. There is a better way: to be more aware of our communication from the start to ensure a greater degree of understanding and a more thorough navigation of expectations.

Is this as simple as it sounds? Assuming ease, being chronically afflicted with "There's nothing to it" sickness, has landed each of us in trouble on more than one occasion. Perhaps you've worked with people who demonstrate little appreciation whatsoever for another's craft and seem to assume that theirs is the only real expertise, everything else being uncomplicated and everyone else stupid. Ignorance, it seems, can be bliss, if you don't mind bombing through life, oblivious to your series of relationship-scorching collisions with others. But serial ignorance and laziness can be expensive—in time, energy, and money—in a big-vision small business that's intent upon developing strong, trusting relationships.

"No one would talk much in society if they knew how often they misunderstood others."

JOHANN WOLFGANG VON GOETHE

Achieving a deeper level of understanding and asking good questions to reveal matched and mismatched expectations relies, again, on self-awareness and skillful listening but carries the possible rewards of richer relationship and freed potential. Such understanding starts with our purposeful adoption of one assumption: that two people in conversation, or several in a group discussion, come to the table with their own particular beliefs, expectations, assumptions, and definitions. The two things we might safely assume are that we can't assume anything and our way of thinking isn't necessarily shared by others.

I remind my employees and myself to see every interaction or meeting as an opportunity to learn something new about the people with whom we're interacting. After a meeting, for example, if we can't point to one or several new things we've learned about the person, we haven't been mindful enough during the meeting. By asking gentle questions and respectfully probing into deeper conversation, whether in the employment interview, ongoing staff meetings and performance evaluations, or discussions with prospective or current clients, we take an important step in building common understanding. This helps to solidify the foundations of right relationship. How? With the assurance of shared expectations, we're less likely to face the prospect of hearing "That's not what I expected" as an employee or client heads out the door.

GOLDEN RULE NO. 5: BE WATCHFUL OF OVERFAMILIARITY

The wonderful thing about developing relationships with others is that we get comfortable interacting with one another and gain a deeper understanding of how others approach things, which allows us to work together more productively and be of greater service. Yet increased familiarity also breeds the possibility for complacency and even sloppy service or a lack of professionalism or respect, whether within the office or between your group and your customers, vendors, or partners.

If the goal of treating others with extraordinary respect and thoughtfulness informs our daily interactions, regardless of whether relationships are new or well established, is it possible to slip into complacency that others might easily perceive as unprofessional or disrespectful? This becomes less likely if, in having extraordinary respect as the goal of our interaction, we're already more mindful of our own behavior in relation to others. Only when we lose sight of our ideal for our interactions—or if we have no ideal, which is too often the case if our predominant interest is meeting profit quotas—are we likely to slip into behavior that distinguishes us in a negative way, if at all.

Our challenge as big-vision small-business owners is to review regularly, in collaboration with the people of our organization, how ideals such as extraordinary respect or the avoidance of overfamiliarity and complacency can inform our actions planned for that day or week. How are we treating one another? How are we treating our clients and vendors? How do we know? Is that good enough? In asking these questions and using the answers to modify and refine our behavior, we move closer to manifesting our highest vision in the enterprise's everyday actions.

Golden Rule No. 6: Foster a Sense of Service and Generosity of Spirit

Many of the business owners with whom I have spoken believe that there are some things you just can't teach a person who isn't open to learning. These lessons are often tempered and shaped in the heat generated by the events of our lives, not taught in a classroom or office building. One such characteristic is having a desire to be of service to others, fostered by a generosity of spirit that can't be contained and seeks outlet at every opportunity—not just during the hour or two of a weekly religious service or the day before a client meeting or performance review.

Such generosity of spirit, a priority of being of service to others, is like the finest gold in any organization, particularly in a small organization that is truly values- and vision-driven. Yet if such a quality isn't teachable to those who don't demonstrate it, how can we as big-vision small-business owners foster it?

This is one of the key challenges we face, one that intersects with our commitment to our organizational vision. Though I believe that everyone on the planet has the capacity for service to others, living, working, and shopping on that planet tells me that not everyone demonstrates such a capacity regularly. And yet, while our culture promotes and celebrates self-service, there are still many people who choose to develop their capacity for generosity to others, including those who choose to do so through their small business. Thus another characteristic that distinguishes the big-vision small business from the pack of mediocre organizations.

Bringing this personal sense of service into a business's fabric, and being committed to that quality as a key component of the business, forces some difficult decisions when recruiting, selecting clients, and determining how big quantitatively the business can be. This is a very individual, very subjective characteristic, so it isn't one we'll find mass-produced and easily acquired. Generosity of spirit and a dedication to service are ways of being, not assembly line activities.

In a big-vision small business we can, through our actions, model these qualities to a greater extent than is possible in a franchise or large company. We can choose to be selective and hire people to whom these traits are also important, versus hiring to meet a numerical quota; we can define, celebrate, and reward demonstrations of such qualities in action; we can do more, rather than less, than what our clients expect; we can share information and resources without nickel-and-diming the recipients; and we can step away from projects or opportunities that would require us to extinguish or subvert such ways of being. These are not easy choices in a world in which success is equated with a bigger number, but they become easier if we have defined our vision and honestly evaluated the priorities that form the foundation of our big-vision small-business ownership.

GOLDEN RULE NO. 7: BE CALM AND CENTERED

I explore the foundational elements of a business owner's ability to remain calm, centered, and skillful in the last section of the book, which covers wisdom and mastery practices. Yet the subject warrants a brief mention as a golden rule. What does one's spiritual or mindset-management practices have to do with one's ability to shine in the area of right relationships? The same thing good soil and attentive care have to do with nurturing a healthy garden.

It doesn't matter whether you call it religion, spirituality, mindset management, philosophy, faith practices, psychology, mind-body wellness, or nothing at all. Many such philosophies provide guidance on how to cultivate ways of being and areas of practice geared to quieting the "anxious mind" and treating people right. Also, if you don't have a set of practices that help you decrease your stress level, reduce your flash points, soften your judgments, and expand your perspective, you are not going to be—or do—as well.

Many studies and books have reached the mainstream regarding how such practices produce more healthful bodies and reduce illness, primarily because they help produce healthier minds. The same is true of your ability to foster right relationships. If you are preoccupied, you cannot listen well and are more likely to be forgetful. If you are angry, you are much less likely to be thinking clearly and speaking respectfully. If you are caught up in fearful thinking, you are more likely to be dwelling on something that hasn't yet happened and less likely to be practicing extraordinary thoughtfulness. Practices such as centering prayer, meditation, exercise, and visualization, for example, help quiet the mind and deepen our faith, thus strengthening the foundation upon which right relationships—and a successful, rewarding livelihood—can be built. (For more information on the relationship between faith and mindset practices and right business, see Section Four.)

Putting the Golden Rules into Practice

So what? you might say. Anyone can adopt these practices regardless of the size of his or her organization, right? And you would be correct in saying so. Yet the things that we *can* do aren't always the things that we choose to do. Think about it. Even if an individual elects to undertake such personal-mastery practices in the area of right relationship, which do you think will be more likely embedded in an organization's culture: a number of individual employees practicing mastery-level communication and relationship building throughout a 4,000- or 85,000-person corporation pressured to achieve a blistering pace of growth and investor return, or every person in a five-person enterprise committed to shared principles and practices for right relationship?

How do these golden rules permeate the very real, very competitive ground on which we do business each day? What might right relationship and extraordinary respect look like in our day-to-day recruiting and managing, in our operations and client service? How might we increase our proficiency in right relationship and develop deep, positive, mutually beneficial connections with employees, customers, and our community? How can we be more conscientious about the effect our business has on others? The remaining chapters in this section feature stories, tips, and insights that have been quilted together from my own and others' experience and offer ideas that we can learn from and incorporate into the daily activities of our big-vision small enterprise.

Chapter 14

CREATING RIGHT RELATIONSHIPS
WITH EMPLOYEES

ONE FRUSTRATION commonly voiced by small-business owners throughout the country is how to find the right people for their small, entrepreneurial, multiple hat–wearing companies. The more specific the vision and its delivery, the less likely it is that just anyone will fit within the organizational culture, particularly in firms that are more a matter of personality type and specialized knowledge than straightforward routine. And so it is with recruitment for a big-vision small business that sets a high bar for right relationship and qualitative growth. How might we incorporate right-relationship principles at the very beginning of our relationships with employees so that we increase the likelihood of making matches with kindred spirits?

While we all know, unfortunately, that a great interview does not necessarily make for a great fit, being as clear as possible before and during the interview can help a business owner bypass a few obvious mismatches. The keys to more effective recruitment include the level of clarity you have about your needs and the type of individual that might be best suited to them, what questions you ask, what information you share, how well you listen, and of course, how well you discern and apply the lessons of the past.

Before the Interview

Know why you're hiring someone new. Why on earth would a business owner hire someone new if the organization didn't need him or her? One possible answer is that she has assumed that quantitative growth is necessary and that, if her group is busy, she should hire additional employees in order to serve the new customers that she should also be seeking. She's "should-happy," which should qualify as a bona fide *disease* rather than as an accepted business practice!

A second possibility is that the business owner may not have assessed whether his group is operating efficiently, making an additional employee a reasonable investment. Is it possible that the existing group actually has the time and skill to handle additional work without jeopardizing a healthy work environment? Would a project-based contractor be more appropriate? Will the new person help the group make the pie bigger, benefiting all members of the organization, or will the result be the same-sized pie with smaller slices (or, Heaven forbid, a smaller pie)? These are questions a business owner might consider before casting the recruitment net for new employees. A big-vision small-business owner asks these questions as an opportunity for reflection and dialogue that will increase his own and his group's awareness, and because he knows both the discussion and the answers will help find the options that best serve the organization's vision.

Marketing Partners' Pat Heffernan of Burlington, Vermont, discusses the decision to increase expenses, whether for new staff members, equipment, or office space, with her employees. Why? So they too can be aware of the decision-making process and help choose the most effective solution. "It's not a 100 percent democratic decision-making process, because if Peg and I feel there's something needed for the viability of the business, we'll get it," says Heffernan. "But often we'll go over it with our staff. All we do is show them how the added expense will affect the year-end bonus pool, which often generates a different level of thinking and problem solving. Many organizations have profit sharing, but there's never any profit. Our group likes to ensure there is a bonus pool at the end of the year, and discussions like this help support that goal."

Know what and whom you need. This seems like a no-brainer, but small-business owners can easily miss or misinterpret this step because they've got a lot of other responsibilities, as well as time and budgeting pressures. Take a few minutes to map out the core values that make your best-fit employees success-ful in your company, as well as a job description that includes key tasks and the traits associated with a person who handles those tasks well.

Doug Hiemstra of Hiemstra Product Development, LLC, in San Francisco found these issues particularly relevant when he recruited for a sales represen-tative for his eight-person design firm. In addition to keeping in mind that his office is fast paced and stressful due to deadlines and the nature of the creative process, Hiemstra had to be clear about whether he needed a marketing spe-cialist or a sales professional. Many people—employers and job hunters alike—don't recognize the difference between the two or aren't aware that they may have conflicting assumptions about what particular job titles mean. "We get a lot of people who offer to be salespeople here, so the challenge is recognizing the true entrepreneurs from the wishful thinkers," he says. "It takes a special personal makeup to be able to get out there and talk to people, to want to get on the phone and call people to schedule meetings. There are people who really prefer to do marketing rather than getting on the phones and overcoming re-jection regularly. So it's key to recognize the necessary personality traits."

Look at what works. If you already have employees, notice what personality traits make someone a good fit for your big-vision small-business culture. Ask good-fit employees why they think they've been successful with your firm, what motivates them about working with the organization, and what sort of person would be most successful on your team. You might be surprised when employ-ees raise insights and concerns you've not considered.

Schedule multiple interviews. Let candidates know up front that you'll be scheduling multiple interviews for all candidates you're considering and pro-vide a specific time frame for your recruitment campaign. "The way we inter-view is important, and we really take a lot of time to hire people," says Craig Galati of Lucchesi, Galati Architects in Las Vegas. Galati takes the first inter-view to talk more generally and determine if a candidate is aligned with the firm's core values. Once that has been established, Galati will move the process forward to discuss capacities and talents and how the prospective employee might benefit the organization. "Some candidates get frustrated that it takes so much time, and we've lost some good people because of that," he says. "But one wrong fit affects everything. In a firm like ours we work in teams that require a lot of collaboration. One person can break that chain for everyone, so we don't want to be in hiring mode. It's known in the community that if you get a job offer from us, it's special. That's how we want it."

Another option to help foster a good fit is to consider having select members of your team do the initial round or two of interviews, making recommendations on the top candidates they think would fit best. If employees are participating in the interviews, make sure they're aware of interview techniques and legal issues before the interviews begin. Once your employees have met with candidates and have forwarded an assessment to you, meet with the candidates yourself. When my own group started conducting interviews this way, we got some very interesting responses from prospective candidates. Several were incensed that they would be meeting first with employees of the company instead of the firm's owners. Their response saved their time and ours, since such that kind of attitude is incompatible with big-vision operating priorities, including our right-relationship practice of being respectful to others regardless of their job title or place in the organizational hierarchy.

Know the value of what you're offering. Value is often associated with monetary offerings compensation and benefit packages, yet there are other factors that make an organization valuable to its employers or customers. Big-vision small businesses offer a number of qualities and benefits unique to their mission, size, area of expertise, and culture. Such qualities rank as high priorities for many prospective employees, particularly in these times, when more and more employees seek meaningful work with socially conscious organizations. Doing a little research and having a dialogue about the value of your organization's offerings can make a big difference in your confidence level and attractiveness to good-fit candidates while serving as a motivation booster within your group.

Many of the big-vision small-business owners I interviewed challenged the stereotype of the typical low-paying small business, for example. While few offered financial compensation at the top of their region's pay scale, most felt compelled to offer financial compensation within a competitive pay range. Says Shelby Putnam Tupper, who has owned her graphic design firm for over a decade, "When a small-business owner says they can't afford reasonable wages, I'd say that raises serious questions about the productivity of their staff or equipment. If they can't pay their employees a livable wage with reasonable benefits, they might not have a viable business. That doesn't mean you don't look for ways to keep costs down, but you don't increase your profit on the backs of your employees."

While reasonable compensation is an important factor in attracting and keeping desirable employees, there are others as well. For example, surveys show that employees enjoy feeling like an integral part of a team and being part of an organization with an inspiring vision and important contribution to society. Employees also say that learning opportunities, positive feedback, and pleasant interpersonal relationships increase their loyalty to a particular employer.

During the Interview

Be realistic. A candidate is more likely to be a good fit if she's worked—happily and productively—in other small-business or entrepreneurial environments. Look for prospective employees whose work history shows a preference for the responsibility, juggling, visibility, and multitasking that come with working for a small business. An alignment with the vision and core values is also important because that's what fuels the passion to take the level of work quality well above the norm—a big-vision small-business priority. The key priority here is to identify opportunities for a mutually beneficial, enjoyable work relationship.

Ask questions that will give you the information you need. A big-vision small-business interview includes careful preparation and thoughtful dialogue. The questions you ask can help you find out whether a person is more comfortable with details or the big picture; is a self-starter or an order taker; thrives on a diverse, ever changing environment or a stable, routine-oriented one; is a positive person who spots the possibilities or a person who focuses more on finding the mistake. These can all be positive or negative traits, depending on the job you need done. Most recruiting ads feature requests for conflicting skills, like asking for a detail-focused accountant who is big-picture oriented or a strategy-minded proofreader. While someone may have honed a level of competence in both, most people are much more effective and efficient in one arena or the other. This is where it's helpful to know what you need and to make sure recruitment ads and interviews clearly communicate those needs. Open-ended questions allow more space for the candidate to share more of his personality, expertise, and way of thinking and being. For example, questions might include:

- What's most important to you about your work?
- What type of work environment do you like the least?
- Knowing what you do about our vision and our work, how do you think you fit with those?
- If hired, how would you like your participation to make a difference in our work and for our customers?

Go with your intuition. Sometimes you can't put into words why someone is or is not clicking with you. If you aren't sure whether to trust your intuition, delay the decision for a day or two until the direction from your instinct becomes clearer. The same rule of delay applies to overwhelming gut-inspired urges to hire a candidate because you like her as a person. A one- or two-day delay allows you to be more certain that your emotional response doesn't result in hiring someone who doesn't have the skills or capacity to be successful in your organization.

Communicate clearly and be gracious. Before, during, and after the interviews, communicate your intentions and progress with each candidate in a timely manner. This is particularly important if your interview process is time-consuming or lengthy. Big-vision small businesses aren't bogged down in process or bureaucracy and thus have an opportunity to excel in thoughtfulness, communication, and right relationship. This extends to your interactions with prospective employees. An added perk? Given the increasing attractiveness of big-vision, socially conscious enterprises among potential employees, your demonstration of big-vision practices in action can serve as a beacon to attract similarly committed, like-spirited employees.

Alternatives to Hiring Full-Time Employees

One big question facing many business owners is when to hire full-time staff members and when to consider other options, such as part-time employees, independent contractors, or partnering with other small businesses. Unfortunately, there's no hard-and-fast rule. The answer depends very much on the business itself, the particular needs, and an awareness of regulatory requirements. The ability to be creative and flexible is an advantage of a smaller, independent enterprise. There are several examples of how this flexibility might present itself.

Several years ago, we at Ivy Sea had a year during which several full-time staff members for a certain job category came and went. An intern on our staff suggested that a graduate student would be more compatible with an organization that was oriented toward learning and continuous improvement, which is how she saw our firm. In her view, people wanting the more settled routine and established outside-work socializing more typical of larger corporations wouldn't mesh well with our independent, mastery-focused group. Students, in contrast, were geared toward learning and would find the firm's dynamic pace and culture exciting.

We took her suggestion to heart. In addition, we expanded our definition of *student* to include candidates who had valuable skills but might be looking, for example, to reenter the job market after graduate school or after having stayed at home with a child or who were making a career shift and wanted to put their skills to use in a new way. We created an advanced internship we call an Ivy Sea Residency. The positions are full- or part-time, finite-term opportunities that can be extended for additional three- or six-month intervals based on discussions of mutual benefit. The positions are compensated fairly, with the high level of learning opportunity taken into account as part of the compensation package. Residents, in return, contribute their skills, and they get an opportunity to reenter the market, as well as to add new marketable skills to their résumés and work samples to their professional portfolios. Based on feedback from participants, the program has been a success, and it has helped us stem the turnover that had previously occurred in that job category.

We've now developed relationships with what we call our "extended family"—a small circle of likeminded professionals with compatible vision, aligned values, and a commitment to rising above the norm in their work. In addition, we maintain contact with a network of other self-employed professionals and small businesses with complementary areas of expertise with whom we partner and exchange referrals. This allows us an experience and expertise pool that is both deep and broad, without having to expand the organization to a degree that would negatively affect our ability to work according to our big-vision priorities and the golden rules for right relationship.

Helen Hempstead of Cor Productions in St. Louis, Missouri, also opts for such partnerships. "We tend to look for people just like us, which means we tend to partner with other entrepreneurial small companies," she says. "While we can do everything from creating a concept, to writing a script, to shooting and editing, we often choose to outsource dubs and duplications to a subcontractor. Whenever we need closed captioning, we work with a business in our network. This way, we're talking to the owner of the firm, and they know how important quality, service, and follow-through are when we give them our project."

Doug Hiemstra takes a similar approach to staffing his product development firm. "While I have eight employees, we're a virtual twelve, because I rely on a network of outside contractors for specific expertise as needed. It works well because we don't need to have those senior-level people on staff full time," says Hiemstra. Even Hiemstra's employees were first independent contractors who worked well enough with Hiemstra and liked his vision enough to join him as his employees. "There's a definite attitude difference with independents, who tend to be problem solvers who get the job done without making excuses," he says. "The people to whom we subcontract are senior-level people who can contribute a lot at the front end of a project as to how to approach a problem. They contribute their expertise as needed for our project and go about running their own businesses."

The latter factor is a crucial one to ensure that you're not tapping contractors who don't meet the independent-contractor qualifications required by the Internal Revenue Service. If you need the person at your office, working regularly month after month on a variety of projects, you probably have an employee, not a contractor. Talk with your accountant or attorney if you're unsure of whether your need is more suited to an employee, a contractor, or a partnership with another small-business owner.

LifeQuest's Barb Banonis is also careful to look for a good values match. "I find out what's in it for them, what they're looking for, and what they love doing, and try to ensure that the project I'm offering them functions around that," she says. "Whether employees or contractors, it's important to collaborate with people who really love doing what you need them to do, and clearly identify your expectations so you're less likely to get bogged down in personality issues."

Once you've made connections with the new members of your team—whether employees, contractors, or aligned-vision partners—you can continue to apply right-relationship practices to help you maintain a work environment and foster work relationships that dovetail with the priorities of a big-vision small business.

Chapter 15

MAINTAINING RIGHT RELATIONSHIPS
WITH EMPLOYEES

FOR THOSE WHO DOUBT the practicality of nurturing right relationships in the workplace, there are many studies connecting such efforts with bottom-line performance. A pleasant, productive workplace is key to employee satisfaction, and employee attitudes are critical to factors such as sales, profitability, customer loyalty, and employee turnover. For example, a Gallup survey of more than 100,000 employees across 12 industries showed the link between communication-related issues—employees knowing their roles, feeling important to the vision and mission of the organization, having a good relationship with their supervisor, being recognized for their work—and organizational success.[3]

Another study by the same group showed that employees are four times more likely to leave the organization if they have a bad manager; and interpersonal and communication issues have been directly linked with management effectiveness and employee satisfaction.[4] The bottom line: pay attention to those operational areas formerly referred to as "soft issues," or you'll be in for some hard, expensive lessons. The good news? Because of their compact size, inspiring vision, and high ideals for making a positive impact on the world in some way, big-vision small enterprises have the potential to excel in these areas. How can you maintain right relationships with the people who help you bring your vision to life? By raising the bar for performance in organizational communication and culture, right from the beginning.

Orientation: Getting Off to a Good Start

To help new employees increase their chances for success in a new job, a big-vision small-business owner must make sure that her organization has an agenda for welcoming, orienting, and mentoring new members of the group. An orientation program doesn't need to be overly complex, expensive, time-consuming, or bureaucratic, but it does need to exist. The approach we've evolved at Ivy Sea, for example, includes a checklist for an orientation process that comprises the predominant share of a new recruit's agenda on his first day at our company. We give him a packet of information that contains concise but information-rich items already reviewed by our attorney, such as: a letter briefly reviewing the position and compensation, accounting paperwork, a job description, a confidentiality agreement, and a "Life at Ivy Sea" handbook.

An Ivy Sea delegate, usually the person to whom the newcomer will report, reviews the contents of the orientation packet, provides necessary instructions, and answers questions and allows the candidate to begin filling out any necessary paperwork and reviewing the other documents. That person also meets with the new team member to review in more detail his job description and initial assignments and takes the newcomer out to lunch to begin the process of welcoming him into our group. His afternoon and subsequent week are spent working on his initial assignments, negotiating more specific performance expectations, and most likely listening in on any project meetings taking place that week—another opportunity to learn how we work and where he might build and contribute other skills.

This minimum level of orientation activity helps ensure that a new staff member—whether part-time or full-time, an industry veteran or entry-level employee—has the building blocks she needs to understand how we work and what we expect. She has the assignments and tools to get right to work contributing her skills.

Following right-relationship tenets, we foresee that the first few weeks at a new job can be very stressful. To the extent that we can think ahead and help someone contribute earlier rather than later allows him to become a part of our group that much sooner. In any group, particularly a small one, feeling like the outsider is not fun. An orientation program helps people become insiders as quickly as possible, and I find that a very organized orientation week supports that goal. We adapt the process for partners and vendors with whom we collaborate, as well.

An orientation program also helps to create clarity from the start and can serve to minimize legal issues that might arise from misinterpretations and differing expectations. But mindfulness about assignments, expectations, and growth opportunities doesn't stop at the orientation. In a big-vision small business that pursues right relationship for qualitative growth, depth is both a priority and an area of distinction—depth in communication, listening, observing, and finding ways to identify, develop, and apply an individual's strengths to the benefit of the organization and its customers. One aspect of depth in right-relationship practice is looking beneath the surface of the job description to find shared understanding, identify areas of high potential, and set the stage for shared responsibility and the cocreation of a positive partnership.

For Great Performance, Get Clear on Roles

Good performance is a shared responsibility that starts with the employer providing an accurate description of the company, work environment, and job and the employee being honest regarding her skills and capacity to do the job. For Carol Conway, president of CRS Technology in Fort Myers, Florida, matching an employee's aptitude with job requirements is crucial to creating a successful work relationship. Given her organization's smaller size, Conway is better able to make such determinations based on personal connection with the employees rather than reliance on tenure or being restricted by hiring policies that exclude otherwise capable employees for lack of certain formal credentials.

I won't put a round peg into a square hole. I don't put field engineers into sales if they prefer to be technical people. And I don't assume all administrative staff members are interested in learning the details about technology systems. It's very important to me, and to the quality of the work environment here, that I let people do what they do best and allow them a lot of latitude within their job responsibilities to create an environment in which they can excel. I think this is just a requirement in a small business rather than some blueprint I create for self-actualization, but it helps when I give employees the parameters of the job and let them create their own performance plans. As a result, the atmosphere here is energized, and my turnover is low.

Too often in a small enterprise, an employee starts a job without any job description other than a verbal summary or vague outline, makes a few assumptions about what her boss wants of her, and finds out what her employer's expectations and preferences are through trial and error. By contrast, in a big-vision small business, everyone is on the lookout for how to best develop, increase and apply individual and group strengths.

To help create the foundation for more successful employment relationships, a big-vision small-business owner can start by meeting with the employee for a more in-depth discussion about the vision, roles within the organization, and expectations of both the owner and the employee. In many companies, what passes for a clear delineation of roles and expectations is anything but, resulting in frustration and unfulfilled potential for both employer and employee. But there are other options to ensure that both you and your employees share a common understanding about goals, expectations, and roles.

Communication and Company Goals

What happens if employers don't provide employees with the information they need to meet the very goals that will determine their own and the company's success? At one organization, employee representatives claimed employees weren't told what the company's goals were, nor did they receive a single progress report. When bonus time arrived and no one received bonuses, employees fought back by voting in a union.

Company expansion also has an effect on communication and culture, primarily because organizational culture becomes more dependent on formal hierarchy, processes, and policies as a company grows in size. This is a reality that Kevin Owens of Select Design, Ltd., in Burlington, Vermont, knows all too well:

For the first three years, we were a typical startup, with two people doing everything from sales and finance to cleaning up. At about eight people, we decided to take a leap of faith, take on more debt and hire salespeople—the biggest commitment period. We devised a more defined management structure when we got to 20 people, with managers for sales, creative work, and production. Now, at 50 people, we're struggling with creating some distance between ourselves as owners from the day-to-day operations, so we can concentrate on strategic issues such as space needs, new markets, and how we give back to the community. Between us partners, we handle nearly 70 percent of the sales in terms of gross dollars, and it's time to let go.

Al Lovata of the 70-plus employee company Be Our Guest agrees that quantitative expansion creates new problems in communication. "Our key questions are about how we structure the organization, how we use technology to help us run more efficiently, and how we communicate the vision and foster the culture as we grow. Three years ago these issues didn't exist, because we could be on top of everything. Now our challenge is how to communicate."

"Few things can help an individual more than to place responsibility on him, and to let him know that you trust him."

BOOKER T. WASHINGTON

Yet even in smaller organizations, unclear goals, roles, and expectations foster higher levels of stress that affect both the employee's performance and the quality of the work relationships and atmosphere. In the worst cases, employee morale and retention sink, and dismissed employees may opt to take legal action. Discord affects teams in all types of organizations, but the negative side effects are all the more evident, and damaging, in a smaller enterprise.

To help alleviate such problems, here are several right relationship–aligned ideas for how you might communicate your big-vision small-enterprise goals more clearly—allowing more productive, better-prepared employees—and come closer to realizing positive results:

· *Relate each goal to employees' jobs and provide tactical action items.* Rather than dictating tactics, engage employees in defining clear, measurable action steps for achieving the goals and contributing their talents.

· *Get goal-achieving ideas from employees.* Use employees' in-depth knowledge of their own jobs to help determine how they can meet or surpass specific goals. For example, you could start by asking, "We want to reduce costs in this area by 12 percent. Where do you see opportunities to do this?"

· *Link company goals to employees' motivators.* If employees have said that bonuses are an important benefit of working at the company, show them how achieving the goals helps them to obtain the bonuses. Ways to do this include sharing individual stories of how someone met a personal goal by working toward company goals. Likewise, since vision, meaningful work, and learning opportunities are significant motivators—even more than financial compensation—engage employees in a dialogue about how their activities connect to the vision and provide opportunities for them to develop deeper skillfulness, experience, and knowledge.

· *Connect goals with activities.* Don't communicate the goals in a vacuum; relate them to everything else going on in the company. For instance, you could include a regular feature in the newsletter or on a bulletin board, share information related to skill development and organizational vision, make links between new projects and the goals, or connect activities with goals at regular staff meetings. This isn't a one-way street—the more you engage members of the team in a discussion, the less the organization resembles a "command and control" hierarchy where everyone awaits orders (and often criticism) from his or her supervisor.

· *Encourage employees to ask questions.* The responsibility for clear understanding of goals rests with both employers and employees, and in a big-vision small business, the group's small size permits more-inclusive, organic communication. If an employer hasn't explained exactly what "achieving world-class service" looks and sounds like, foster an environment where employees own responsibility for asking for clarification—thus applying the golden rule for checking assumptions, for example. Foster an environment where everyone respectfully challenges empty jargon, opting instead for clear communication and mutual understanding. For example, an employee might ask, "Since my performance review requires 'good customer service,' what kind of examples will you look for to determine whether I've met that goal?" or, "What does 'being reliable' or 'supporting the sales goals' look and sound like to you?" Make such inquiries part of an employee's job description and a requirement for successful performance.

As the firm's leader, take responsibility for providing specific examples of what goal-supportive performance is, just as you lead the way in modeling the behaviors you're looking to encourage in your group.

While these tips cover just a fraction of the organizational and interpersonal communication skills required when discussing goals, they do shine a light on everyone's responsibility in adopting right-relationship practices to help the big-vision small business achieve its goals.

Performance Evaluation and Recognition

While most employees certainly expect fair financial compensation, nonfinancial forms of recognition often prove more motivating. Surveys show that employees value worthwhile work, learning opportunities, clear roles, feedback about progress, and good old-fashioned appreciation for a job well done, as well as fair pay.[5]

Recognition can take many forms in a big-vision small business, from increased responsibility and special assignments to fun gifts or public kudos. Some firms reward mission-supportive performance with on-the-spot gift certificates for movies, videos, books, restaurants, groceries, or the local coffeehouse or spa. Other companies invite employees to assess and reward their peers with "all hands" e-mails or other communications touting their fellow employee's positive behavior. According to employees, the peer approval is highly valued. Also, by recognizing peers, employees are underscoring for themselves and others what the goals are—and how on a daily basis they can achieve them. Other culture-promoting recognition options include tuition for professional development courses or workshops, an unexpected day off or team outing to the baseball park. While enterprises of all sizes can offer most of these perks, a big-vision small business—given its personal connections and lack of bureaucracy—can better fulfill what is for many employees a key need: to feel like they're an integral part of an organization that is doing meaningful work in the world in a way that makes everyone associated feel proud and offers many opportunities for growth.

These kinds of recognition don't negate the option of providing financial rewards, such as annual merit or profit-sharing bonuses. While pay-for-performance programs are ubiquitous in management discussion circles, they are not universally revered.[6] Not everyone thinks that such plans promote productivity or build loyalty—a belief reinforced in California's Silicon Valley, where financial reward was the sole focus of many fast-growth, wealth-focused dot-com and high-tech recruitment efforts—and employee turnover was reported to hover as high as an astounding 75 percent.[7] The more the companies made their recruitment campaigns about "be fast, get rich," the less loyalty they engendered among their employees, who were in turn stung and demoralized when the companies collapsed as funding ran out and there was no real vision or mission to propel it onward.

While not wanting to create a company culture obsessed with individual interests and "get rich quick" wealth accumulation, most big-vision small-business owners do want to share some portion of the profit with employees. The difference? Choosing a reward system that reinforces qualitative growth, vision alignment, organization culture norms, and performance goals over individual self-interest.

Regardless of the goals you establish together or the forms of recognition you adopt, provide frequent updates to employees on their progress toward achieving mutually established goals, and provide clear feedback regarding required improvements. In most big-vision small businesses, performance discussions occur much more frequently than the annual evaluations common to most large corporations. One option is to meet with each employee on a monthly basis to identify progress toward his goals and opportunities for continued improvement. Because you're communicating about performance expectations and progress regularly, employees are more aware of how they're doing, and you can link recognition to those efforts that support individual and company goals.

Ending Relationships That Are No Longer Mutually Beneficial

According to the tenets of right relationship, true compassion requires that you take the appropriate action to change a relationship when it becomes evident that an employee is not a good fit in your company culture or for the needs of the business. This might include a recent hire, a vendor, or someone who has been with your company for a longer time but no longer has the interests, skills, or preferences that are compatible with your business.

"The difficult thing for small business, and for myself as a solo practitioner, is that by working in isolation we can be operating with our patterns getting the best of us because it's hard to correct one's self," says Lawrence Ellis, founding principal of Lawrence Ellis & Associates and founding convener of the Paths to Change network. "In smaller or solo enterprises, you can very easily get locked into routines that reinforce your shortcomings. In large organizations there is a different kind of learning disability, though, where the system continues to reward you for not learning how to learn from your mistakes."

A big-vision small-business owner develops a network and process to ensure her own continuous learning so that she expands beyond limiting patterns—her life and business are, in this way, a work in progress. Where someone else's learning is concerned, she realizes that sometimes the best and kindest decision is to let someone go elsewhere to find a new environment in which he or she can grow and flourish. Such people can more easily linger on in a large organization with a dysfunctional culture, where an ill-matched employee might simply be worked around or transferred into another department as a way to avoid conflict or confrontation. In a small business that is operating according to big-vision priorities and right-relationship principles, mismatches are evident more immediately and approached honestly and respectfully.

Sometimes the best and kindest decision is to let someone go elsewhere to find a new environment in which he or she can grow and flourish.

"I don't mind firing someone if we're moving in different directions," says Bill Myers, of Ithaca, New York–based Alternatives Federal Credit Union. "I see other organizations where people let mismatches hang on for years, to the detriment of everyone involved. We try to give people as generous a severance package as is justifiable and wish them well on their way, but we don't delay for sentimental reasons. It doesn't serve anyone to be in the wrong position." Myers says his years as a manager have given him the confidence to identify and take action in those situations where an individual is clearly no longer suited to the organization. "Less experienced managers often feel like it's their failure if they can't make it work out," he says. "That's just not how I see it anymore. I want to validate an individual as a person and not repudiate the time they've been with us. I'm more comfortable talking about what our future will be and what their future will be and emphasizing that we just won't be moving into those futures together."

Part of validating an individual—and a requirement for right relationship—is to try to identify a mutually respectful conclusion to the employment relationship so that the circumstances might make a foundation for positive momentum. Ideally, if there is no other option but to terminate the employment relationship, a big-vision small-business owner would revisit the golden rules and right-relationship tenets and engage the employee in a dialogue about the situation, including concerns and potential opportunities or next steps. As a result, he would have improved the likelihood of a continued relationship, potential future collaboration, or at the very least, the employee's being positive ambassadors for the business.

Chapter 16

CREATING RIGHT RELATIONSHIPS
WITH CUSTOMERS

MAINTAINING STRONG, integrity-based re-
lationships with clients is no different than maintaining right relationships
with anyone else. There are large corporations, such as Nordstrom, and
Hewlett-Packard with their "HP Way," that subscribe to high ideals for employee relations and customer service. Such companies set the benchmark for
other larger organizations, particularly when contrasted with less impressive
corporate performance norms. In a big-vision small business, customer relationship can be cultivated to a higher degree of personalization and mastery
than in companies whose intense focus on fast growth and high profit margins
renders relationship a lesser priority.

A big-vision small-business owner sees relationship cultivation from the
perspective of a master craftsman, so that the possibilities take her and her
group to a level well beyond simple jargon masking the mediocre. A customer
relationship can be strengthened by communicating skillfully and respectfully;
checking in on progress, performance, and expectations regularly; delivering
quality products and services that match the client's expectations; following
through on promises or being up-front about why you can't; providing excellent
response when things go wrong; and being thoughtful about ways to increase
the value of your services to the client without unduly increasing costs or ignoring your own bottom line.

"Some businesses treat customers as job orders and not as relationships. When I focus on building relationships, the jobs come and referrals are made," says Jill Erickson, whose Milwaukee-based company, Create A Scene, designs murals for restaurants, retail spaces, and private residences. While artistic talent is a critical part of Erickson's exchange with clients, her attention to right relationships is a nonnegotiable aspect of her business and one reason she's gained the respect of both clients and peers. "It boils down to how I'd want to be treated. If I was that client, what would I want? They don't want to be imposed upon by the stereotypical artist attitude," she says of the often temperamental or unprofessional interactions commonly associated with some of the more creative trades. "In return, I make sure the client values my services and pays a fair fee, because not everyone understands the effort that goes into the painting process. Honoring myself at that same time is another way of honoring my clients."

Erickson's focus on respectful interactions and mutually beneficial experiences provides a good example of the balance required in creating and maintaining right relationships with customers—a key component of not just a healthy bottom line but a rewarding livelihood as well. The larger an organization and the more prominent its focus on fast growth or maximized investor return, the greater the pressure to view customers as commodities that one must amass in the most efficient way in order to meet quarterly earnings projections and thus receive a more positive rating from Wall Street analysts. In a small-scale enterprise focused on deep connection as a pathway to qualitative growth and success, financial viability serves right relationships, not the other way around.

Right Relationships Begin before the Sale

In the average enterprise, many vendor-client relationships sour due to a gap between expectations created through the marketing hype and the customer's experience with the firm. In a big-vision small business, the bar is set high for customer relationships. To foster such a master-craftsman level of right relationship with customers, you have to start with your marketing and sales approach.

Selling is a form of communication, and business owners must sell their products and services in order to reach and communicate with those who can benefit from their work. Unfortunately, many companies invest far too little time making sure that the marketing and sales communications are clear, that the interactions are reflective of the organization's vision, and that promises made are in line with what the customer experiences. Many companies communicate one thing to entice the customer to buy their products and services yet deliver something quite different once they've made the sale. A big-vision small business works to bridge that gap, leveraging the big-vision priorities, applying the golden rules for right relationship, and using some of the following techniques to foster healthy, mutually beneficial connections.

Know your products and your services—and why they're of value to your customers. Effective salespeople sell from the heart, or at least from their vision; they genuinely believe that the client would benefit from the product or service. They know the product and (to a certain extent) the client, inside and out. This knowledge allows the successful salesperson to address questions and concerns while maintaining confidence about the ability to help someone else.

For you the business owner, if you can't articulate your company's merits, persuade a client to trust you, and energize someone else about the power of your product or service, how can you effectively serve the client and your own organization's goals? A good salesperson knows she has to make the contact, build the relationship, and gain her client's confidence before she can begin helping that client meet his goal. This is where knowing the advantages and contributions of small business—shared earlier in Section One—becomes all the more important. The same is true for effectively communicating how the big-vision operating priorities benefit the customer.

Know your audience and speak their language. Truly effective salespeople tailor the information they provide to their audience or prospective client. This sounds deceptively simple. Unfortunately, many marketing and sales communications—whether presented on paper, in person, or via the Web—are presented through the filters of their creators rather than tailored to the interests and needs of their recipients. What's more, such communications can be so laden with meaningless jargon that the materials are useless because they fail to distinguish what they'll actually do for the customer in comparison to competitors. A small business has the advantage of being able to make a deeper, more personalized connection with the customer, so don't sabotage that advantage by using indifferent language. Jargon doesn't always make you seem smarter. Sometimes it just makes you sound like you're from another planet— and one for which the customer doesn't have (or want) a language decoder.

Discover your prospective client's primary issues, needs, or goals. Through solid research (Web, print, conversations, or interviews), identify how your services can help the person(s) achieve goals, meet needs, or resolve issues. In doing so, you've shifted your mindset from "Must make the sale; must complete the tactic" to the user-focused "How might our product or service truly help this group work better and meet its goals?"

Ask questions and listen. You've probably heard the saying "When you open your mouth, your ears slam shut." It's true, and good salespeople know it. Only when you understand the client's needs can you know how your services might benefit her. Selling does not equal talking. Two common mistakes: talking too much and describing how you can help before you've gathered adequate information. By applying several of the golden rules that help develop better listening and interaction skills, big-vision small-business representatives try to make every communication an opportunity to learn more about the customer and share information and expertise that helps the customer solve a problem or identify and enhance a strength (which no doubt solves another problem).

Do you ever provide the boilerplate solutions that are common to large companies? (I hope you're shuddering at that thought.) No, you listen and ask questions to find out what a particular client needs. This technique can also help you build a strong rapport with the client and increase his or her confidence in the expertise your company offers—another area where a big-vision small business can shine with master-craftsman quality.

Focus on benefits, not just features. Even sales and marketing professionals often focus more on what they've got to sell than how their products or services can legitimately benefit the client. Perhaps this is one of the dangers of having a focus solely on numerical goals and the pressure of meeting fast-growth quotas, where an "I have to sell you" mentality makes the features more important. If you're going to help your client live or work more joyfully and effectively, you'll need to show how your products and services can help them meet both qualitative and quantitative goals, deadlines, and the expectations of their superiors in the organization. A benefits-focused approach answers the question "So what good does this do me?" A big-vision small-business approach also includes "How can this make life and work more enjoyable and meaningful?"

Know your purpose and your limits. This is pretty straightforward, but often learned the hard way. Remember the big-vision priority, featured in Section Two, about working to a higher degree of ethics and integrity? Regardless of your good intentions, fabulous service ethic, and great roster of services or products, if you aren't the best person (or company) to meet your prospective customer's needs for whatever reason, say so. Then build a team of people who can or refer the client to another source. An appropriate referral can be a great sales tool because the prospective client will remember that you were interested in meeting her needs rather than making your sales quota. You've treated her in accordance with the tenets of right relationship, making her a person instead of rendering her a commodity. Determining which projects are inappropriate and which are potential opportunities for expansion is much easier if you're checking in regularly with your vision and business plan.

Once you've earned your customer's business, you have a wonderful opportunity to demonstrate the advantages of her choice to purchase products or services from a big-vision small business. The opportunities for qualitative growth and high-bar performance don't end with the sale but transition into the next phase of the relationship by satisfying common expectations and determining how to go beyond the mediocre.

Common Expectations

One of the most important factors in creating a strong foundation with a new customer or for a new project is solidifying a common understanding of expectations and deliverables. Think it's easy? If so, you're very likely making the same assumptions as most people who end up saying, "I should have made that clearer at the start." Don't assume your customer knows how you work, what to expect, or what you'll deliver.

Many high-potential relationships fail because participants assume that, because they're using the same words and nodding their heads, they're translating those words into common expectations. One of the complaints we hear during assessments we've conducted for client companies is that they need to do a better job of clearly and proactively communicating expectations and processes at the beginning of a project, and of keeping customers informed about progress. Too many customers shoulder the responsibility of calling the vendor for updates and fail to get what they expected because expectations were never made clear.

Let the big-vision priorities and golden rules serve to guide you. As you begin a new project or relationship, discuss in explicit terms what the client will be getting, and what his needs are regarding communication and service throughout the process:

- What's made her happy or dissatisfied with previous projects undertaken by other vendors or merchants?
- What would have to happen to make sure he's able to give you rave reviews upon completion of the project?
- Does she want daily or weekly progress reports?
- Would he prefer those updates by telephone, e-mail, or fax?
- When does she feel in-person meetings are necessary or appropriate?
- Does he agree with your proposed delivery dates?
- Are you two in sync about what will be delivered and how?
- Have you discussed how your company works on such projects?
- Have you discussed, specifically, what you need from her and her team to produce your end of the project agreement?
- Does he know what responsibilities you and he each have to create a successful outcome and a good relationship that continues past the project delivery date?
- Have you introduced him to the members of your team who'll be contributing to his project?

How might you adapt these questions to your particular type of client interaction, whether you own a consulting firm, a retail store, or a restaurant? Regardless of your company focus or industry, building right relationships is a mutual responsibility for which you can be a guide. Establishing common expectations and understanding right from the start will help create a positive relationship and experience for both the customer and the people of your company, and thus help you make the most of each opportunity for qualitative growth.

Now that you've gotten the relationship with a new customer off to a great start, use your master-craftsman standards to sustain and revitalize that connection, as well as optimize service to new and existing customers. The next chapter offers food for reflection and dialogue on maintaining big-vision right relationships with clients.

Chapter 17

Maintaining Right Relationships
with Customers

You have surely had experiences with a company for which the clear priority was getting, not keeping, your business. You know the usual clues revealing a lack of respect for the customer—long wait times, overworked customer-service representatives, lack of empowerment to solve problems, late or unavailable merchandise, messes left behind by workers, inaccessible account representatives.

Worse, there is that emerging trend *Civilization* magazine called "prosuming," where you "let your customers work for you," doing the work formerly done by paid employees. The article pointed to software, banking, and express-delivery industries, where customers are doing more online and by telephone (checking their accounts, paying bills, placing orders, and the like), as spearheading this new trend.[8] Such approaches are suited to very large enterprises that rely on technology and efficiency processes to sustain massive size and hyperaggressive growth rates.

Perhaps needless to say, for big-vision small-business owners, the prosumer model of customer relations seems both unethical and undesirable. So how can you apply the big-vision standard for right relationship in a way that leverages the potential advantages of small enterprise and benefits everyone involved?

Attention to Detail

While being mindful and detail-oriented at the beginning of a project or relationship helps considerably in getting you off to a good start, the proof is in the delivery. Whether your relationship with clients extends over longer-term consulting projects or shorter bursts of contact when customers make a retail purchase, they will remember whether their interaction with you was convenient or inconvenient, encouraging or disheartening, personalized or sterile, frustrating or fluid. What are you doing, specifically, to ensure that your client's experience with your business is convenient, encouraging and smooth, and therefore repeated and referred?

Some small-business owners identify the negative customer-experience norms within their industry and put into place practices that offer just the opposite. For example, Iris Harrell of Harrell Remodeling knew only too well what a typical construction customer experiences during the course of an average project: rudeness, foul language, litter on the property, loud music, missed deadlines, and a lack of communication. Just as her employment practices run counter to industry norms, Harrell's client-service practices include an assurance that employees working on a specific project will refrain from using foul language and listening to music while at the customer's site, will pick up all debris and litter, and will update the client regularly as to the project's status. Harrell's customers aren't put in the position of having to work hard to work with her firm, as is the case with many companies professing a commitment to "customer care" that seems to end once they've secured the business.

Bruce Hetrick of Indianapolis-based Hetrick Communications advises all of his clients to participate in regularly scheduled update meetings to generate discussion and build a common understanding of expectations throughout the life of a project. While not all clients agree to the meetings, Hetrick feels it is his responsibility to communicate the benefits of doing so and sees fewer miscommunications and greater satisfaction in the cases where clients do participate.

One of the small things we at Ivy Sea try to do routinely is to keep our clients' interests in mind as we go through the workday, so we can pass along relevant journals, Web site addresses, or other resources or information that the client may find helpful. When we find such information, which is often, we don't bill for the time spent reading or surfing nor charge the client for the purchase price of a journal or a photocopy of an Ivy Sea article, for example. While this sounds simple, it's customary in consulting and professional services to bill for everything, including phone calls, photocopies, faxes, and any time spent thinking about the client. We've opted to structure our fees by project and make sure that our fees are adequate, so we can provide for the details without nickel-and-diming our client. Our priority is keeping our client in mind outside of the requirements of a specific project, which makes for pleasant—and lengthy—relationships that extend beyond the life of that project.

Leaving Things as You Find Them

When we moved into new office space in late 1998, we hired several vendors to do work related to the build-out, such as painting, opening doorways, and installing heating, ventilation, and air-conditioning systems. We acted on our commitment to hire small businesses for all the work and dealt with the owners or senior representatives. Since the vendors performed their work in tandem, we witnessed a marked contrast in how the professed dedication to customer service played out as the work was done and the projects wrapped. All were pleasant to deal with at the project negotiation stage. Once the work began, the companies became more distinguished. The contrast offers but one example of the difference between mediocre or average enterprise and big-vision performance.

In the best case, one vendor's workers arrived as scheduled and conducted the work within the time frame and budget negotiated. I received a call to verify their arrival and revisit expectations regarding what they were doing and when. The crew finished up and the foreman politely checked with me on whether it would be a disruption if they vacuumed and cleaned the space and told me how long that would take. As promised, the crew left the work space as clean as it was upon their arrival, the only evidence of their presence being the doorway they installed. I then received a call from my original contact verifying that the project met my expectations. Start to finish, it was an excellent interaction that gave the impression the vendor cared about the quality of the customer's experience with his firm. As a result, we've confidently referred the firm to several colleagues.

In the case of the other firms, the workers were disruptive, talking loudly and, in one case, interrupting staff members to inquire whether we'd turn on the radio since the office was too quiet for her. One worker routinely interrupted a nearby employee for casual conversation and sat down to use a telephone without asking, while another arrived late and then powered up a concrete drill while a staff member was on the telephone with a client. The projects took longer than scheduled, and our office was left with drywall and concrete dust on computer equipment, in addition to paint spattered on the carpet. Upon calling the owner of one of the firms, I was told to take a razor blade to cut up the paint spatter and then steam clean the carpets. We did our own vacuuming and dusting as well.

For me, these experiences served as a reminder of a key right-relationship rule: be very conscious of the impact your services or work has on the customer, particularly if you're working in the customer's space. Practically speaking, demonstrating mindfulness might include:

- Communicating specifically when you'll be arriving to do work
- Verifying when you've mailed, faxed, or e-mailed something
- Letting the customer know ahead of time if your work will require something of them or whether it will be disruptive so they may plan accordingly
- Checking in upon arrival to let the customer know you're there and what your work will require that day
- Not making your customer guess what you're doing or whether they can conduct business that day (in our example, the delay in schedule and resultant unexpected noise during work hours significantly disrupted our ability to conduct scheduled business and telephone meetings)
- Leaving things as you found them. Don't rearrange furniture, equipment, or trash cans. Don't leave litter or debris from your work in the work space.
- Not interrupting the customer unless you've arranged to do so in advance. If you'll need customer feedback during your work, arrange

this before you arrive so that they can adjust their schedule to accommodate you. The same goes for noise or other environmental disruptions.

You can easily adapt or expand this list based on how the people of your company routinely interact with customers. For example, even if you're not physically working at a customer's site, you enter their space with your phone calls, e-mails, and deliverables, and you enter their minds when you do or do not anticipate their needs or follow through on your promises. In a restaurant or coffee shop, you can demonstrate consideration by anticipating needs, being polite and welcoming if not friendly, following through in a timely manner, getting orders right, being flexible to meet special requests, and expressing gratitude for the customer's business. All of these gestures help create a more positive interaction that demonstrates your knowledge that you can affect someone's day for better or worse. In a big-vision small enterprise, we endeavor to make it better.

The primary result of being mindful is minimizing any negative or inconvenient effects of your delivery so the customer can focus completely on receiving the desired outcome consistent with—or exceeding—their expectations. At Ivy Sea, we remind ourselves regularly that our customers don't contact us looking for more stress and hassle; we want to make sure we're the one thing in their day they do not have to battle with or worry about.

Reality Checks

Many companies, large and small, conduct periodic surveys with clients to ensure satisfaction. Surveys can be valuable, but their effectiveness depends largely on the quality of the questions and the listening skills of the interviewer. In some cases, as with written multiple-choice surveys, there is no opportunity for personal interaction or to ask clarifying and probing questions. While quantitative surveys are certainly useful when statistical data is your goal, qualitative surveys are far more effective for a relationship-driven big-vision business intent upon using the data gleaned to improve customer-interaction practices.

A good example is offered by an electronic newsletter that I received, which featured a sample customer-satisfaction survey readers could use to "delight customers." The seven-question survey included measures such as "Rate the quality of our customer care" and "To what extent would you recommend our services?" This particular survey was a good example of how such an effort can skim the surface by using vague language and yes-or-no questions and miss excellent opportunities for deepening the relationship and gaining truly useful information. Why do I say this? The survey questions might yield an answer, such as "Customer care is fair," that provides no specific details about what, specifically, your company is doing from the customer's perspective to seem caring or uncaring or to warrant a referral or not. The survey satisfied a quantitative goal—"do survey," *check!*—rather than providing information to allow for qualitative growth, including improved service through refined behaviors and attitudes, more skillful interactions, and better follow-through.

It's easy to catch the "vapid jargon disease" prevalent in the business world because it's so contagious, flowing in a torrent from seemingly wise management and leadership books.[9] Remember, for example, the ubiquitous use of "world-class service," "best of breed," and "delighting your customer" verbiage? Best of breed? What's horrid about that terminology is that few of the users were running dog shows, for which the wording might be appropriate. And then there are the other two vacant phrases. Unless you know exactly what you mean by *world-class service* and *delighting your customer* and have information regarding what specifically delights your customer—and if, in fact, your customer is delighted (or wants to be)—you won't be "delighting" your customers consistently. Perhaps the more practical and enjoyable goal would be to commit to respectful interactions, consistency, good communication, and follow-through and delivery of the products and services you've promised in a manner that's convenient and satisfying for the customer. A poor survey made up of such superficial questions not only costs a lot of money and gives you information you can't act upon but wastes your customers' time—hardly something most would find delightful. However, statistical surveys are more convenient and provide information that more readily satisfies quantitative goals.

In a small-scale enterprise where there is a different balance between qualitative and quantitative goals, a qualitative survey is more relevant because it allows you to continue successful behaviors and activities while creating a plan to refine areas of weakness and identify opportunities for qualitative growth.

Customer surveys might be more valuable if they contain open-ended questions and an opportunity to delve more deeply into answers. This would allow you to define what's most important to the customer and whether the interactions with your company are delivering just that. Instead of sending out a multiple-choice survey, for example, with questions such as "Did you find your recent experience with us delightful?" or "Was your experience with us fair, good, or excellent?" you might schedule 15-minute discussions with customers to find out what they value most about your products and services, what they wouldn't want you to stop doing, and what's most important to them when purchasing products and services such as yours. One good way to get constructive criticism that many people avoid is to ask, "If you absolutely had to select at least two things that would have made your experience with us better, what would they be?" That gives you more specific, actionable information than general surveys.

Once you have that information, you can make whatever adjustments are necessary in your delivery or interaction practices to consistently make customer experiences positive—and be much more likely to "delight" your customers. But what about those occasions when the relationship is no longer mutually beneficial, when one or the other of you no longer feels valued or delighted?

When Parting Ways Is the Right Choice

While some relationships evolve and strengthen over the years, many are more situational or short-term based on timing, need, or other shifting circumstances. As with the case of employee tenure, seeing relationship turnover as an opportunity can be difficult, particularly for business owners to whom lengthy relationships are a measure of pride and success (which pretty much includes most of us). How might a big-vision small-business owner approach troubled client relationships or end the customer-vendor relationship in a skillful manner?

"There's a tendency when you first start a business to take every customer or client who walks in the door, and that can be a real problem when you upgrade your business and have to take action on the unprofitable accounts," says Sandy Collins of Collins and Mason CPAs in Oakland, California. Being more mindful at the start, even while seeking to meet quantitative goals, may help avoid problems at a later point in the relationship. "If business owners are more selective in the beginning, they don't run into those problems," says Collins. "But in most cases, they're so anxious to get the client that they don't adequately screen or turn away inappropriate opportunities, and those can become the accounts from hell."

In other situations, a customer's needs may be a good match for your organization's particular services, products, or expertise, and the relationship simply outgrows its usefulness. In some of these cases, the relationship moves past its healthy end point because neither party wants or feels able to take the action needed to disengage. The result? Not only is the relationship no longer mutually beneficial—a key component of right relationship—but one or both parties become increasingly disadvantaged and the relationship becomes increasingly inefficient, taking even more time and resources to maintain in its unhealthy state.

In a very large organization, highly irritated customers may go without finding resolution to complaints for extended periods of time, with the company buffered by seemingly impermeable voicemail systems and frontline customer-service agents who have the responsibility to field the complaints but don't always have the authority to make amends in a timely manner, if at all. In a small enterprise that relies on relationship and reputation, hiding places are all but nonexistent, particularly if your service area is more local and the likelihood of running into disgruntled customers is high. This visibility acts as a check and balance for the small enterprise. On one hand, it encourages better service and responsiveness before a problem occurs. If a problem does arise, on the other hand, there is more of an impetus to find a solution that pleases the client in some way, and there exists a greater ability to make a quick decision without working up a hierarchy for approval.

As Collins suggests, being more careful at the start of the relationship by following the golden rules and other big-vision priorities can make it easier to bring relationships to a less awkward end. Beginning the same relationship more complacently allows for vagueness that can ultimately lead to conflict.

WHY DO CLIENT RELATIONSHIPS DETERIORATE?

How can you manage a relationship that is no longer mutually beneficial? Begin by briefly exploring just a few of the reasons you may have allowed the relationship to overstep its boundaries.

You didn't trust your instincts. You've no doubt had experiences in which you acted against the gnawing in your gut that's trying to help you avoid a mistake. You don't heed the voice of your intuition or instinct and end up with a situation that isn't optimal or even remotely pleasant. Were you so focused on quantitative growth that you missed signs of potential trouble, a mismatch between your values and their needs, or opportunities for clarification about expectations?

You thought you needed the business to survive. This may have been true. At some points during the course of running a business, you may take projects or accounts that aren't aligned with your ideal customer profile simply because the business helps pay the bills while you're getting established or changing course. That's reasonable, as long as the rules of engagement and service are clear from the start. Even in such cases, you can work in accordance with your big-vision values and right-relationship style to make the experience a mutually beneficial one. But in other cases, the voice that says "You'll never get another client, so you better take this one" is no longer appropriate. Your task? Moving beyond that fear and creating the opportunities that are more suited to your interests and the current state of your business. Another opportunity for qualitative growth! (Didn't I say that owning a big-vision small business can be a pathway to personal development?)

You weren't clear at the start of the relationship. We've already reviewed the importance of mindfulness and skillful communication in getting relationships off to a good start, so we have no need to revisit the concept in depth. Still, it's one possibility if you're in a client relationship that has become dysfunctional.

You're avoiding confrontation and conflict. Is it possible that your overextended or awkward client relationships get to that point because you don't have a more skillful means of raising issues like fairness, boundaries, late payments, disrespectful behavior, and similar aspects of unhealthy client relationships?

Every time we avoid discussing such issues as they arise, it gets harder to rectify the situation and maintain a more positive, mutually beneficial relationship.[10]

TAKING ACTION ON TROUBLED CLIENT RELATIONSHIPS

Ultimately, damaged relationships will end. The question is, if we're endeavoring to act in a respectful manner toward those with whom we interact, how can we either get the relationship back on track or end it in as positive a way as possible? The right set of tactics depends on the specific situation, but here are a few possible approaches:

Reflect on what brought the relationship to this point. No one is served by your rewriting history or refusing to see your own complicity in creating an undesirable situation. The same is true of failing to recognize, truthfully, the other party's contributions to the unraveling of the relationship. Neither of these practices helps to foster qualitative growth and right relationship. Sit down, alone or with your group, for an honest, respectful dialogue and outline the key issues and actions that brought you to the present, as well as potential solutions that can lead to ethical, healthful closure. Make it an opportunity for revisiting the vision, values, and optimal standards that guide your group's everyday work.

Have a dialogue with the customer. Regardless of how uncomfortable you may be with confrontation or conflict, the only other alternative is to let an unhealthy (and probably disrespectful) situation continue until it comes to its own sputtering or explosive demise. Engaging the client in dialogue engages your energy and resources in a beneficial way, since it allows learning that can be used immediately thereafter, as well as an opportunity to preserve a relationship that will otherwise be unsalvageable. In contrast, letting problems fester consumes your energy and resources, casts a pall over your work environment, provides a negative example to employees, and may very well jeopardize your reputation. Once you've outlined the issues, actions, and potential solutions with your group, call the client to schedule a time for constructive dialogue. Share your intention for resolving what you believe is a situation of concern to all parties.

Be prepared and reinforce your interest in a mutually beneficial solution. Your meeting with your customer provides an opportunity for you to share your perceptions and concerns about what's happened with the relationship, but it doesn't end there. Remember the big-vision priority for mutual benefit? As a dialogue, the meeting will also afford your customer an opportunity to speak his mind about where and why the relationship unraveled. In fact, you'll want to use the golden rules to ask gentle questions and create an atmosphere that encourages sharing perspectives. Listening may be a challenge for all parties, so the best place to begin your discussion is with an agreement about highest intentions and mutually beneficial solutions. Establishing those as your meeting ideals will serve as an anchor during a potentially difficult discussion.

As for turning away inappropriate business opportunities, one way to approach the situation with an intention for right relationship is to provide alternatives to the prospective customer. For example, you might keep a roster of other providers you feel comfortable referring business to who provide similar or peripheral products or services. Another option that goes beyond just saying "no" to a prospective client is to spend a few minutes on the telephone to identify the person's real need. In some cases, a person who has contacted you may come looking for one thing but needing another that falls into your area of service after all. In other cases, it will help you provide a more qualified referral option. Either way, instead of an abrupt disconnect, you're creating an opportunity to be of service to the prospective customer and your referral network.

Finding the Energy—or Inspiration— for Practicing Right Relationship

What motivates someone to have big-vision small-business priorities and pursue right relationship, leverage a small-business asset, and accomplish qualitative growth? It does seem, after all, as though it would be a heck of a lot easier to just run the average business like most people do (that's what makes it average). Why would you want to create extra work for yourself? And even if you go the big-vision route, where do you get the fuel to sustain such an approach?

The Economist magazine, in a special section dedicated to entrepreneurs, quipped that entrepreneurs may be a delusional lot in their quest to do the impossible without regard to what's normal or a care for what's easy.[11] A qualitative entrepreneur herself, Dawn Rivers Baker asks, "What kind of a mind do you have to have to play this game?" Baker is the founder of Wahmpreneur Publishing, Inc., which provides political advocacy and publishes business information "for people who work where they live."[12] "Among the lessons which life teaches, the small business owner knows that nothing really worthwhile is easy and that success is that much sweeter when it is that much more difficult to come by," she offers. "If more people understood that, many of the social ills that plague us would largely disappear."

This belief motivates a big-vision, small-business owner to go beyond quick wealth accumulation and instant gratification, despite cultural pressures to do otherwise. The very purpose of one's focus on pursuing qualitative growth and *enough* financial well-being is making a more meaningful contribution to something beyond one's own business and to someone other than oneself. From where do such beliefs originate? Big-vision small-business owners often find both their inspiration— and a means of sustenance—in their faith, wisdom, or mastery practices. The next section offers dialogue, ideas, insights, and reflections on just what that might mean.

> *"We won't always know whose lives we touched and made better for our having cared, because actions can sometimes have unforeseen ramifications. What's important is that you do care and you act."*
>
> CHARLOTTE LUNSFORD,
> COMMUNITY SERVICE
> LEADER

KEY №. 4:
TO LIVE FROM
THE SOURCE,
REPLENISH
THE WELL

"Without divine assistance

I cannot succeed; with it

I cannot fail."

Abraham Lincoln

Chapter 18

WISDOM AND MASTERY IN BUSINESS

WHAT DO WISDOM, faith, and mastery have to do with small business? If you've gleaned anything from the preceding chapters, you know at least one thing: taking the qualitative growth, big-vision small-business path can be very challenging and thus requires inspiration, faith, mastery, and wisdom—sometimes in very large doses.

While life as an employee includes the more trying moments that can broaden perspective, wisdom, and skillfulness, someone else ultimately holds the responsibility for ensuring that the business remains viable (and for seeing that the garbage cans get emptied). A small-business owner, in contrast, has many of the same personal and professional responsibilities as his employees yet also walks the bottom line as the enterprise's primary investor, decision maker, risk taker, and accountability holder. Add the higher standards and ideals of creating and sustaining a business aligned with big-vision priorities and practices, and the crowd begins to thin.

This is why a big-vision small enterprise can be a powerful vehicle for personal, professional, and spiritual development. Most wisdom and mastery schools include right relationship, right view or vision, compassionate communication, courage, service to others, and other big-vision principles among their primary tenets. To emphasize them as points of excellence and distinction in your business is to make them high priorities for refinement and development. This section begins an exploration of the symbiotic relationship between wisdom, mastery, and big-vision small business and how that relationship offers fertile ground for qualitative growth.

Wisdom, Faith, Mastery, and Business

Historical accounts suggest that Abraham Lincoln—who was, you may remember, the coproprietor of a small law practice before he became president of the United States—suffered great bouts of melancholy and depression. At times while he was president, he was said to be mentally and spiritually wounded by the ills that breached the nation and by the decisions he, as the embattled republic's leader, routinely had to make.

Lincoln was not a fair-weather leader; he governed during far from easy times. Despite the fact that his words would become etched in the nation's memory and moral fabric, many of his decisions were publicly ridiculed and vigorously opposed by many of the journalists and politicians of his day (including those who alleged that he scribbled out the now acclaimed Gettysburg Address while on a train to the next political speech). From where did he draw the strength to endure the difficulties of leadership? With what did he shore up his surely challenged faith?

Leaders from the far reaches of history to the present day have drawn much needed inspiration from a variety of wisdom and mastery practices. What is the role, then, of such practices in the health of a visionary small-business leader and, in turn, the healthy evolution and contribution of her business? Regardless of the words used—*faith, spirituality, religion, philosophy, mindset management, psychology, personal development*—some sort of practice, often philosophical or spiritual in nature, forms the basis for a business owner's ability to skillfully envision and implement her business—and then navigate the challenges of business ownership. In turn, the journey of business ownership has the potential to become a vehicle or form of ministry through which one practices and builds competence, knowledge, and wisdom. As contemporary theologian and author Matthew Fox writes in his book *The Reinvention of Work,* "Work is that which puts us in touch with others, not so much at the level of personal interaction, but at the level of service in the community."[1]

For his part, Marcus Aurelius, philosopher and emperor of Rome, relied on the teachings of Stoic philosophers to help him maintain clarity, integrity, purposefulness, and perspective during the two turbulent decades of his leadership.[2] Many modern-day leaders find guidance in the teachings of Aurelius and others like him as they strive to live and work with faith and integrity in a world that remains turbulent.

Personal mastery practices, while perhaps drawing from a well that includes philosophical and faith teachings, seem to address more tactical measures for making externally visible changes, where wisdom practices emphasize change from within. On one hand, well-known personal-mastery experts such as Anthony Robbins inspire motivation in their followers through a dynamic presentation style, generous doses of real-world anecdotes, and step-by-step "do it to become it" processes. Faith leaders or spiritual gurus, on the other hand, emphasize a "believe it to see it" approach that incorporates practices such as meditation, prayer, and sacred readings. Tapping psychologically based personal-mastery practices in the workplace doesn't often raise eyebrows. After all, applying Anthony Robbins's teachings or the mindset management approaches of your favorite professional athletes doesn't cross the line we draw between public and private, religious and secular. Start talking about religion or spirituality at work, and more than a few hackles are raised. A big-vision small-business practice draws upon resources from both wells.

What Is the Role of Faith Practices in Our Work?

Many philosophical and spiritual belief systems include guidance for how one's ethics or values might become manifest in one's work. Buddhists refer to right livelihood, Christians may refer to the work or calling, Judaism includes the path of the Baal Shem Tov, Islam influences how its most mindful followers work, as do the Tao, Baha'i, Native American Church, and other guiding faith practices or philosophical approaches.

The European Baha'i Business Forum (EBBF), for example, embraces a very deliberate mission, with aligned core values, to integrate the Baha'i faith practices with the business activities of its members. Similar in spirit to other faith and wisdom traditions, EBBF seeks to promote several core values or concepts:[3]

1. Ethical business practices
2. The social responsibility of business

3. Stewardship of the earth's resources

4. Partnership of women and men in all fields of endeavor

5. The need to redefine the meaning of work

6. Nonadversarial decision making through consultation

7. The application of spiritual principles, or human values, to the solution of economic problems

According to George Starcher of EBBF, "The statement of our mission has helped enormously to motivate an increasing number of members to be active in promoting and practicing values such as business ethics and corporate social responsibility in a number of ways. Some members organize and participate in monthly meetings in Paris, Amsterdam, Zurich, and other places, with speakers on one or another of the core values."

Other EBBF members, Starcher relates, have made dramatic, sometimes life-changing decisions as a result of their participation in EBBF and their commitment to living these values:

One member was an asset manager for a bank in Luxembourg and left to become a management consultant because he felt advising clients on investing money held for tax evasion or other unethical reasons was morally wrong. Still other members struggle to practice these values on a day-to-day basis in their own companies: one member turned down a $20 million contract because he sincerely felt the behavior of the client did not permit him to add real value to the project. Finally, one of our Russian members owns an advertising agency and asks candidates he is recruiting to read and accept our core values. One candidate said he agreed to all of the values except he could not agree to equal opportunity for women and men. He was not hired as a result.

Followers of varying faith or philosophical practices who take these belief systems to heart find themselves, sometimes unexpectedly, on the common ground of running their small enterprise in a way that is more conscious of its effect on others; keeps one's family, community, and world in mind; and is in some way of service to the health and sustenance of the whole system or group through the work of the individual. And there is value in drawing from a practice other than one's own. Though I'm not a practicing Buddhist, for instance, reading about the Buddha's Eightfold Path or Four Noble Truths has been both educational and inspiring,

with its encouragement of right relationship and right action. While it's very chal-
lenging to consistently meet such high ideals, the wisdom is very relevant to the
way I want to run my business and do my work. Other small-business owners feel
the same way about martial arts or similar disciplines that align practices for
mind, body, and spirit with the intention of being a more enlightened citizen in
business as well as private life.

Faith and the Marketplace: Old or New Trend?

Mixing wisdom practices and work is hardly a new trend, though you might think it so, judging from the flurry of "soul of the corporation" books hitting the market in recent years. In fact, the very words *professional, vocation,* and *money* have distinctly spiritual historical roots or affiliations. The word *professional* has referred to one who professes his faith; *vocation* has historically spoken of divine calling; and the word *money* is derived from Monéta, also known as Juno, in whose temple ancient Romans housed their mint.[4] Even *Forbes* magazine had more idealistic origins than one would guess. B. C. Forbes started the publication in 1917 with the primary intention of encouraging humaneness in the business community, which he felt was "mercenarily minded, obsessed only with determination to roll up profits regardless of the suicidal consequences of their shortsighted conduct."[5]

Many people still create distinct separations between religious or faith practices and the work they do for a living: one set of practices occurs in their church, temple, or mosque; another set of practices is relegated to the workplace; and perhaps still another is reserved for the home. Yet many an individual proudly speaks of her "Puritan work ethic," in which idle hands breed the devil's work and industriousness is righteous, without giving a thought to the concept's spiritual roots. People often seem unaware of how deeply their worldview of work and business is connected to the religious practices of some of their country's—and culture's—very pious founding mothers and fathers.

Still, an increasing number of us, whether small-business owners or employees, are more openly discussing and quietly incorporating the connection between our faith or mastery practices and how we work or conduct business.

Why are we so fearful about connecting spiritual and business activities, and how can we find a positive, authentic balance between the two?

Where Religion and Work Meet

The appropriate place for faith practices in our highly pragmatic business world is a delicate issue. Such activities can easily go beyond a quiet source of inspiration for ethical practices to become mandated or, perhaps worse, appropriated by a company for questionable—if not decidedly unspiritual or unethical—purposes.

Why the growing interest, or concern, about the intersection of spirituality with work? The corporation is requiring increasing amounts of an employee's time. American workers put in more hours per year than do their counterparts in other industrialized nations. And with some companies offering assistance with what used to be very personal responsibilities—everything from laundry pickup to day care to dinner takeout, and even corporation-paid chaplains—is it any surprise that prayer circles or readings from the world's holy scriptures might take place in a corporate conference room instead of the church hall or someone's living room?

As is the case with many management trends, a key challenge is seeing that valuable, and in this case sacred, concepts or traditions don't become shallow buzz phrases that mask less than honorable corporate actions. In the best cases, leaders embrace these activities because they serve the highest good of the men and women who work for the organization. But many "spirit at work" practices can seem more like well-meaning but reflection-free efforts that insult deeply held faith traditions and threaten to create unhealthy dependencies.

For example, one company's much publicized program of sending employees off on Native American–style vision quests so they can have breakthrough thinking on new product development seems a shameful step over a very sacred line.[6] However, it's a step that more and more corporations will take if it promises to extract one more drop of creativity that can be used to boost investor return. Corporate executives walk a fine line between promoting practices that they hope will increase employee productivity and retention and taking care not to favor religious activity in situations that could be seen as prejudicial. What if an employee felt penalized because he did not share the openly practiced faith traditions of his manager or refused to go on a "vision quest" in protest over the perceived disrespectful nature of such a program?

Exploitation of the renewed interest in spirituality can also be found in corporate advertising—such as television commercials depicting spiritual gurus, angels, or meditation groups as a means to sell hamburgers, office equipment, or financial services. By creating a connection to the viewers' desire for spiritual progress, the advertisers suggest that the product or service in question can help achieve a more spiritual state—a twist that implies you can skip the more demanding meditation practice and simply eat your way to spiritual enlightenment by stuffing yourself with a deluxe burger and french fries while driving your luxury car. Who cares that the actual tenets of such spiritual traditions are aimed at getting you past the very same material obsessions?

"You can't take our beliefs out of the Badlands and put them into one of your factories or office buildings."

JOHN (FIRE) LAME DEER, SIOUX MEDICINE MAN

In contrast to the efforts of their public-company counterparts, leaders in private organizations may have greater leeway in encouraging ethics or faith practices that would be heavily scrutinized in a public corporation. In some private companies, chief executives encourage ways of working that are inspired by their Christian practices, referring to God or Jesus Christ as their chief executive officer. Others speak openly of the role their personal faith traditions play in their work life and business priorities and open business meetings with a prayer. In a big-vision enterprise, where everyone is invited to work in accordance to his own and the organization's shared values, such practices might be welcomed so long as they're introduced respectfully and no one is required to adopt the spiritual beliefs of a colleague or employer. Indeed, in some big-vision organizations, the emphasis is on a set of virtues or values rather than on the rituals of a particular religion.

Clarks is one enduring organization that has operated in accordance with the founding family's Quaker roots since its inception in 1825. The British shoe company credits its long-term success to the Quaker propensity for "plain dealing"—having integrity in dealings with others and generally striving to be above reproach. The result is a lean operation that has a respected reputation for social responsibility, progressive employment and manufacturing policies, and high-quality products that have become even more popular in an era of the "geek chic" dress code favored in technology companies.[7]

In another example that is now almost legendary, Aaron Feuerstein, the president and chief executive of Malden Mills Industries, Inc., in Lawrence, Massachusetts, chose to rebuild his factory after fire closed the operation in December 1995. In addition to making an announcement of that commitment immediately after the fire, he made a second very unusual decision that eased the deep anxiety no doubt felt by the company's 3,000 employees: all would receive full pay for 90 days and benefits for twice that time. The story is legendary because, judging from contemporary news headlines, most company executives wouldn't make such a costly decision even if the company's financial situation made it possible. But Feuerstein did, referencing the Torah as his source of inspiration, citing a teaching that "not everybody who makes money is wise in the eyes of God" and that a good name, earned by decent behavior and caring for others, is the greatest treasure that one can acquire.[8]

As for employees, while those of a small business don't share the identical concerns and challenges of their large-corporation counterparts, they are challenged nonetheless to find meaning in their work. A small business can be an optimal learning laboratory for an employee who prefers a more intimate, familylike, merit-based dynamic, and who disdains unnecessary bureaucracy, hierarchy, and tenure-based promotion. Yet the same employee may occasionally feel the pressure of being very visible, on good days and bad, and feel the weight of the responsibility that comes with being crucial to the organization. She must struggle on some days to make that discomfort worthwhile. And the demands of business ownership only multiply and magnify the need to find meaning. This is one issue where big-vision priorities and practices can help: answering the question "Why is this worthwhile?"

Even with more talk of spirituality on the job, ardently espousing religious beliefs in the workplace makes many people uncomfortable. This may be due to a sensitivity to anything that resembles the enforcement of certain religious practices in a country where religious freedom is protected by the Constitution and where a general sense of freedom is both an individual and entrepreneurial priority. There certainly seems cause for concern when faith traditions are mined and stripped of their spiritual intent for use by the corporation toward what some feel are dubious ends that run counter to the underlying tenets of the religious practice harvested. And yet there is middle ground between, on one hand, mandated religious activity or disrespectful misuse of faith practices and, on the other, having no relationship between spiritual practice and one's work. You can find inspiration in such practices as a source of renewal that fuels and provides guidance about how to implement the big vision.

One hurdle is language and the assumptions that certain words generate. Fervent attachment or aversion to specific definitions of words such as *faith* (and certainly *God*) may prevent any possibilities for a symbiosis of faith practices and secular work. In the spirit of the golden rules featured in Section Three, relinquish even for a moment your preconceived notions about faith, wisdom traditions, religion, spirituality, and personal-mastery practices. Hold an open mind and heart as we explore and reflect upon possible options for an appropriate relationship between such activities and our work as big-vision small-enterprise owners.

The Need for Meaning in the Workplace

Regardless of the discomfort it may cause, it's an important discussion. With the downsizing and intense market fluctuation of the recent decade, we're in the midst of a crisis of meaning. More and more people talk openly of needing more balance and less work-related stress, renewing or building ties to communities outside of work, cultivating greater meaning and skillfulness in their work, and seeking limits on just how much of their time and energy the corporation owns. According to a 2000 Gallup study, 80 percent of Americans feel the need for spiritual growth. Numerous other studies link intrinsic motivation and performance quality; the more individually meaningful the assignment or job, the more satisfied the participant and the better his performance. Another study discusses the ability of study participants to find meaning in even the most repetitive, seemingly mundane work by taking pride in doing the job well or linking the job to how it benefits others.[9]

Given the number of hours spent working and the fact that meaning makes work more satisfying, it's no wonder that more people are seeking a greater purpose. Nor is it surprising that the interest in self-help, personal mastery, and spiritual books, workshops, and practices has been on the rise in the same decade that saw enormous corporate shake-ups, downsizings, mergers, and layoffs (not to mention significant business and political ethics scandals). Their faith in the Almighty Corporation shaken, more people are returning to the teachings and practices that have endured beyond the life of the most recent initial public offering (IPO) or market cycle. Some seekers find more stability and a greater sense of meaning in the arms of the ancient sacred teachings than they found while wrapped in the false security blanket of their employer company.

Wisdom traditions have been associated with and valued for fostering a sense of purpose in the daily tasks that make up a meaningful life. The wisdom embodied in such traditions helps answer the questions What gives you meaning or a sense of purpose? Can something external to you *give* you that sense, or is harboring such an expectation merely setting yourself up for misery? How does a sense of meaning or purpose help us navigate difficult times?

Since faith and personal mastery practices foster meaning in the hearts and minds of the faithful, these disciplines, personally inspired and individually practiced, can be highly relevant to our own performance in and the sense of purpose we derive from (and share through) our big-vision small business.

Common Wisdom and Mindset Challenges

Business and its inherent challenges seem highly practical concerns, particularly when viewed through a cultural filter that emphasizes quantity as an absolute measure for success. Yet there is, as any business owner can tell you, much about business that is anything but tangible. There is no logical answer, for example, why a business owner might choose to persevere, at a financial cost to himself, when the odds of staying in business seem heavily stacked against him. Similarly, it seems irrational to the hard-core profiteer that a big-vision business owner would reduce her own financial return on investment in favor of a higher ratio of charitable work, a more selective client roster, a less profitable but personally satisfying business niche, a noble cause, more time with family, or other seemingly "mushy" pursuits. Such decisions don't fit the prevailing business model because they rely on a definition of value that includes qualitative as well as quantitative priorities. Money is one—but not the only or even most important—factor in the big-vision small-business bottom line.

Each of us nurtures a whole stable of expectations and perceptions that lead to anxiety over our societal insistence that business should be an absolutely linear affair that neatly conforms to a spreadsheet analysis. Although some business leaders think otherwise, business is not a completely mechanical, rational, or tangible matter, precisely because it involves human beings and relies to some degree on an unseen dynamic that even philosopher-economist Adam Smith acknowledged as "the invisible hand" or "code of honor." We arrogantly believe that we can and should control everything and suffer because we cannot. For example, what makes us think that everything should be easy and that, if something is challenging or difficult, there must be something wrong, either with us or the situation? Similarly, faced with common business challenges, such as those that occur in staffing, financing, or business development, why can we be immediately beset by embarrassment, anxiety, or feelings of failure that can likely be traced not to our own interest but to our concern over how we're perceived by others? How can we pursue the high ideals of a big-vision enterprise if we're so easily thrown off course by more mundane challenges?

Mindset management plays an enormous role in how we define our business and its role in our lives, just as it does in how we respond to a host of related hurdles and external pressures. And if thought is the realm of spirituality and psychology, then wisdom traditions and personal-mastery practices are the ultimate prescription for such ills.

Remember, one of the things that differentiates the big-vision small-business owner from his peers is how he faces and works through issues about money, risk, competition, balance, time, and success (to name a few) and what he does when confronted by these opportunities for qualitative growth. Let's take a look at just a few of the issues that challenge our perceptions and, depending on our wisdom and understanding, may sometimes cause considerable anxiety (and potential for mastery) in an average small-business owner's week.

Chapter 19

MONEY AND RISK

THERE ARE A GOOD NUMBER of business owners who, when asked about money, say with pride that they've never borrowed money or owed a dime while building their business. While I appreciate the feeling of being debt free and have found immense satisfaction in my own bootstrap moments, this mindset is potentially limiting, particularly with regard to business. Since small enterprises don't often have the backup resources afforded to larger corporations, how we as owners approach the issue of money and risk is crucial if we're to pursue a big-vision small business way of operating.

The fact is, many small-business owners manage their business finances not much differently than they manage their personal finances—or even manage them seemingly backward. Whereas many people are perfectly comfortable borrowing tens or hundreds of thousands of dollars for a car or home that could be reduced to scrap in a matter of minutes, or sitting in a classroom for several years to earn a degree that may or may not turn out to be useful, fewer are comfortable borrowing a fraction as much to build and learn through their business. I mention these not to suggest that a home or academic degree is less valuable than a business but rather to establish the sharp contradictions in how people view risk and assign value to things. A small-business owner might casually talk about his $400,000 mortgage but look nauseated if asked if he'd borrow that much to develop his enterprise.

A humorous bit of advice regarding risk and money comes from Paul Hawken in one of my favorite practical business books, *Growing a Business*. Along with some other practical gems, Hawken tells a story about one of his own forays into business financing, where he concluded that the best thing to do, in his experience, was either borrow big or not at all.[10] The gist? When you're in for a sizeable sum of money to a specific lender, they're less likely to call the loan and more likely to treat you better than they might if you were a much smaller borrower. Of course, you have to know your threshold—the amount that constitutes "big" for you—and have both the skill to adeptly manage the debt and the iron stomach necessary to deal with the risk without making yourself physically and mentally ill.

But what exactly is risk, and why is taking risks such a big deal when money and material possessions are at stake? A business adviser of mine recently said that risk doesn't mean you lose all your money and belongings but that you're comfortable with volatility. When risk relates to finances, I'd add that, in addition to comfort with volatility, you have to have confidence in your ability to responsibly manage the debt and create ways of paying it off. And you have to believe in your business if you're going to find the energy and inspiration to propel you through one valley to the next peak.

Another reason for pause regarding risk is that, in our culture, risk takers are glorified (when they're seen as succeeding) or vilified (when they're seen as failing), so perhaps it's not too surprising that taking risks, despite being glamorized, still isn't easy for many people.

In talking with a wide variety of business owners about money, debt, and risk and thinking through my own experiences with these issues, I've realized that the fear is rooted in perception and mindset. In cases where someone has a high level of anxiety about money or debt or of fear caused by perceived risks, how often is the issue really about external perception: "What would others think of me if I had to sell my luxury car or big house for more modest ones?" In cases where individuals have a higher comfort with volatility and more confidence in their ability to either avoid or deal with any negative consequences, borrowing money, being in debt, and paying it off is simply a routine part of business. For these business owners, it's more a matter of integrity, ingenuity, and commitment than it is a cause for extreme stress.

"I think many small-business people start a business from their house, so they impose their household budget and household ability to borrow," says Jim Amaral, a baker who founded Borealis Breads in Wells, Maine, which now has four locations. "In New England, there's a mindset that you don't borrow money. But in this day and age, with the business market changing as quickly as it does, even when you're talking about a basic necessity like making bread, it'd be hard to run a business without financing."

For Amaral and other business owners, myself included, taking on the risk of business debt to finance the evolution of the company can have an unexpected benefit. In addition to funding growth and developing your credit history, debt, like feelings of obligation to those who count on you for employment or expertise, can be a real motivator to persevere through challenges that might otherwise cause you to quit or settle beneath your potential. For the duration of the debt, you have to find ways to make the business more viable, efficient, and profitable so you can honor your agreement to repay the loan. In doing so, you realize where you've been lazy and complacent and where you have underestimated not only your own and your employees' ability but also the value of your product or service. That process can have undeniably stressful moments—my own personal threshold making itself evident in one night of insomnia when I was frozen with what seemed like white-cold terror coursing through my veins that we wouldn't be able to repay our loans. Despite such moments, you have the opportunity to focus, recommit yourself to your big-vision adventure, and creatively "work the problem" to emerge through it more confident and mature about your priorities and business acumen. A big-vision small-enterprise owner would not recklessly pursue debt but would recognize that responsible financing may be both necessary and beneficial.

Why are money and the risks associated with it such a cause of stress in Western culture? Perhaps because we too often believe that we should have more than we do, thus allowing us to buy more of everything—from cars to homes to gadgets to employees to happiness—than we currently have. This raises at least two good questions we might ask as we reflect on issues of business evolution and financing: what exactly is wrong with what we have at any given moment? And what makes us think that having more will make us feel better?

The answer to the first question is subject to personal reflection, though I'd suggest that the ubiquitous nature of psychologically manipulative advertising deserves some fault (or credit, if you're in advertising). Just take a look around you. The purpose of almost every commercial, Internet banner, billboard, radio, television, or print advertisement is to play on your insecurities and make you think that you'll feel better after you've purchased the product in question. And you may, briefly. Unfortunately, the elixir of "new" evaporates quickly, leaving you vulnerable to the next wave of not so subtle suggestions about what you lack and why you'll feel better once you've bought it. While advertising is a business and cultural reality, being asleep to its effect on you is neither healthy nor wise. And this provides context for a response to the second question: incessantly desiring that which you don't have is a key cause of misery and suffering, and so is the insatiable pursuit of perpetually escalating quantities of material wealth.

Every ancient wisdom tradition suggests the former, and recent research verifies the latter. According to numerous studies by Richard Ryan and Tim Kasser, professors of psychology at the University of Rochester and Knox College in Illinois, respectively, individuals who seek satisfaction through material wealth or status symbols, be it money or cars or beauty, have a higher degree of anxiety and depression; are more likely to use substances such as alcohol, cigarettes, or drugs; and have greater problems creating lasting relationships.[11] This research strongly suggests that the age-old maxim is true: Money can't buy happiness or health.

For big-vision small-business owners, faith and wisdom practices help you to appreciate what you have and to know what is enough, making you less vulnerable to the very powerful forces compelling you toward mindless acquisition or accomplishments that in the end mean nothing to you. That doesn't mean you stop setting goals or buying products. You just don't expect a goal based on someone else's standard of success, or a material object of any price, to provide a sense of worth and fulfillment that can only originate from within.

Chapter 20

COMPETITION

ANOTHER MINDSET CHALLENGE for a big-vision small-business owner is how we approach the concept of competition. Competition is as American as baseball and apple pie and so ingrained in every stratum of life that questioning how we think about competition almost seems blasphemous. In the most positive sense, competition can propel us to higher levels of performance and service and create the friction needed for personal and organizational evolution. And yet mindless competition can have negative consequences, particularly when virtues such as honesty, integrity, and fairness get set aside in the rush to win and "beat the competition."

The 2000 U.S. presidential election offers one visible consequence of unmitigated, unmindful competition in the all-out war to win at any cost, and I'm not talking about the candidates. On election night, major news networks—reporting results as voting polls in the United States closed—prematurely predicted that Vice President Al Gore was the winner in the state of Florida, retracted that report as new information came in, and then made yet another erroneous call in favor of George W. Bush later that evening. In the early hours of the next day, the networks were forced to retract that prediction as well. Although the typical efforts to lay blame for the seemingly irresponsible and hugely consequential mistake ensued, so did discussion regarding the reason behind the networks' rush to judgment in reporting the returns.

"The networks today . . . are under phenomenal competitive pressures," explained Marvin Kalb, executive director of the Joan Shorenstein Center on the Press, Politics and Public Policy, in an interview with Terrence Smith on *The NewsHour with Jim Lehrer* the day after the election. Kalb said that, as a result of this intense competitive pressure, the networks make such decisions "based on ratings, on money, on a determination to succeed, sometimes even without regard to the quest for facts and accuracy."[12]

News, like sports, has become big business, and both are very prominent examples of our cultural brainwashing, which dissociates competition from qualitative virtues such as ethics, integrity, and civility. Small-business owners are no less susceptible to the strong public messaging, whether through news headlines or well-distributed management theory, that in order to be successful, you must be paranoid (in the words of one well-known chief executive) and actively strategizing ways to "crush your competition." Add these messages to those of the current gaggle of management gurus warning that you must "grow or die" and do it "urgently," and you can see where worries about surviving your competition take root. While it's certainly fine to pay attention to current management theory and peruse the day's headlines, big-vision small-enterprise owners know that it is also wise to keep it all in proper perspective. Just review and weigh whether it's appropriate to your vision and individual priorities and whether it's even relevant as a strategy for your business.

For one thing, do you really need to "destroy" or "kill" your competition, in the violent and outdated battlespeak of one generation of business executives, or might it actually be more productive to shift from butchering your competition to refining your own offerings and enhancing your overall impact on all stakeholders? Steven Carter shares a wonderful story about this in his book *Integrity*, in which he tells of a student council election campaign in which he refused to engage in negative tactics and didn't even mention his opponent's name.[13]

Following this model, your sense of competitiveness is then not so much discarded as it is refocused, becoming a matter of competing against your own past and current big-vision standards of service and product quality. In this approach, while you pay attention to what similar companies might be doing, you spend more of your time and energy talking to past, current, and prospective customers about their interests, needs, and perspectives on what might make your company unique and therefore preferable to them. This isn't new information—there is no shortage of published material on either customer service or competition—but it is a modification of your perspective and priorities as a small-business owner. After all, most information published about issues such as competition, growth, and customer service is based on the norms of the very large, not small, business.

For example, leadership books or conferences featuring the growth of a 1,000-employee software company or an 85,000-employee megacorporation are barely, if at all, relevant to a three-person independent bookstore, a six-person consulting firm, a 20-member construction company, or even a 50-employee candy-manufacturing operation. While the latter may find lessons about upgrading the manufacturing process, all might be better served by studying organizations that are more similar in size and service area, gathering input from customers and employees, and sharing wisdom with peer business owners to sharpen competitive performance.

Another significant concern regarding competition, at least for many small-business owners, is how to position your business and successfully coexist in the presence of, and sometimes right next door to, megacorporations or chain stores. In some cases, owners of a small enterprise adopt an indignant attitude and stubbornly cling to their previous ways of doing business, assuming that their customers *should* support them by virtue of the fact that they are local independent enterprises.

Needless to say, while this approach might feel righteous for a short while, it's not an optimal or realistic business strategy. Nor does it leverage big-vision small-business practices. There are areas where small, independent, big-vision enterprises can perform extraordinarily well in contrast to their clunkier, more homogeneous chain or colossal counterparts. To resist proactively weaving an awareness of small-business attributes into your mindset and business strategy is like partnering with these same corporate giants to guarantee your company's demise. Though a well-run small business can still fail because of the chain that moved across the street, there are plenty of examples in which a healthy viewpoint toward competition and a sharp awareness of the unique capabilities of a smaller organization have allowed a business owner to carve a niche and survive the arrival of the Big Guys. Just ask Mike Sheldrake, big-vision owner of Polly's Gourmet Coffee in Long Beach, California.

Sheldrake bought the coffee store in 1989, in a neighborhood then known for its row of independent boutiques and shops. Less than a decade later, the neighborhood was transforming due to the arrival of multiple chain stores. Clothing, book, and finally coffee chains found their way to the Belmont Shores shopping district, and Sheldrake watched as several local independent businesses fell behind and ultimately went out of business because, from his perspective, they refused to change their marketing approach and refine their niche. "The arrival of the chain stores raises the expectation level; they raise the bar for performance," says Sheldrake. "So you have to run your business in a professional manner and give your employees the resources they need to be very good at their jobs. That can be a challenge for some small-business people: needing to have a professional demeanor and a higher standard of operation. If you're there by yourself, you may not be held to the same standard of accountability."

"The arrival of the chain stores raises the expectation level; they raise the bar for performance."

MIKE SHELDRAKE

Instead of wasting valuable time simply complaining about the chain stores—although he is an outspoken champion of small business—Sheldrake made it a priority to observe what the chain coffee stores offered and how they did business. And then he got busy on a strategy to refine his operation by focusing on opportunities for qualitative growth. "The first thing I did was realize the importance of image and marketing. It's all perception," says Sheldrake. "I'm good at operations, so I hired a marketing consultant, who did a survey."

Sheldrake's strategy to refine and redefine his niche included making investments in employee training, facility upgrading, and marketing. "We had to train our staff to work at a higher standard of customer service, and we compensated them for those standards. We also had to rebuild our facility to reflect why people come to our store: we roast our own coffee and offer a warm, personalized environment. And we redefined ourselves in contrast to the chains, which offer 'ordinary coffee.' As a result of the program, 71 percent of the people we surveyed recognize our advertising slogan."

And while Sheldrake knew very well what competing coffee chains were offering, his shifts in strategy focused more on his customers' needs and preferences and then making sure that his business was doing a high-quality job meeting those standards. The mistake some other small-business owners made was falling into a stubborn insistence that their customers should come to them because they were not a chain. This is evidence of mediocre rather than big-vision thinking. In response, Sheldrake again emphasizes the higher standard of professionalism and service mandated by the presence of the chain stores. "When you walk into one of the independently owned stores, the money you put on the counter is money you've worked hard for. It's incumbent upon that small-business merchant to ensure you're given value for your purchase. It's an attitude, a degree of professionalism," says Sheldrake, that distinguishes the big-vision small business from many other small businesses.

Unfortunately, that attitude of high-caliber service and a more refined level of professionalism seem absent in many small enterprises. Despite their potential for uniqueness, the failure to respect the customer contributes to their demise, particularly in the face of well-financed chain operations that seem like small businesses to some customers. So adopting an attitude of "They should come to us because we're small businesses" fails miserably, not just from a bottom-line standpoint but from a perspective of right relationship as well. For the big-vision, small-business owner, however, it's an opportunity to develop wisdom and mastery by choosing to refine and shine. "The solution is finding a niche where you can service the customer better than the Big Guy," advises Sheldrake. "For example, we have a wider variety of giftware and coffee, and we have a well-trained staff."

Sheldrake says that the presence of the business owner, a local resident, can also be an enormous edge. "It's a great advantage that the owner is there in the business. With the Big Guy, everyone's trying to please the guy above him. They are big and well financed, they're professional, and they're not going away. If I screw up, I go out of business and lose everything, and they take the business. On the other hand, if I do my job properly, they can't touch me, because as a small business I can offer things they can't do as well."

One important perspective to keep in mind regarding competition as it relates to very small enterprises is that you don't need to engage every prospective client out there. And if you've capped quantitative growth in favor of a smaller, high-quality, big-vision operation, there is a limit to the number of customers you can serve and still maintain your standards of interaction and service. What's more, if you have certain requirements regarding quality of life, you have to acknowledge that some prospective clients are not good matches, for any number of reasons, with your organization.

What *do* you need to be concerned with? I suggest it's this: how many customers you can serve in order to meet your profit *and* service goals, how your organization is unique, how you'll go about fulfilling your promises of service and product quality, and how that best serves the needs of your niche of customers and enhances your community in a way that benefits all participants.

Chapter 21

SUCCESS AND FAILURE

ISN'T IT AMAZING how a person can go through life thinking he's attending to important things like a good little boy, vying to succeed in the way success is defined, only to find in the face of his impending death that his view of reality is horribly skewed? Physician, researcher, and author Dr. Elisabeth Kübler Ross, and others who have spent years working with people who are dying, have repeatedly heard what people regret about their life as they face death. Guess what? The regrets of dying human beings, when they've got time to think about it, are far more about qualitative matters than quantitative things. Most worry not about the promotion they didn't get, the deal they didn't do, the number of employees they didn't have, the stock they didn't purchase, or the car they didn't buy but about the way they didn't act, the people they didn't serve, the relationships they didn't build, and the things they didn't say.

The dilemma is not that setting and driving toward goals or enjoying the material fruits of our labors is something deplorable but more that we view these as "The Point" rather than a vehicle which we can, toward the end of our lives, believe has been truly valuable. In a big-vision small business, we can and should take care of the quantitative matters —payroll, revenues, profits, and the like—not as an end in and of themselves but to foster viability that, in return, allows us to somehow be of service or do something of real value in our world. And we can define our success accordingly.

"I know I shouldn't compare myself to others," says Wendi Gilbert, partner with her husband, Paul, in San Francisco's Heart at Work Productions. "You just don't know what someone else's goals are or whether they're truly successful. They don't wear or share their struggles or challenges, necessarily, so what you see isn't the whole story. Comparing your business to someone else's is okay for marketing information but not for making a decision about whether your business is successful. That has to be measured according to your own goals." What's more, adds Paul, "Once they become relatively successful, people tend to forget the struggles and glamorize those early or lean times, when it's those challenges that probably taught them more about success. As a business owner, the reality is that you have to keep trying, and maintain a perspective that there are no real successes or failures— everything is just a learning experience."

> *"When I'm looking for senior management, if they have nothing but successes, that scares the heck out of me. I want someone who's seen it all, who's ridden the rocket up and down. Because you learn a lot more coming down."*
>
> BRUCE FERNIE,
> FOUNDER AND CHAIRMAN,
> TEALUXE INC., BOSTON

Many people make the mistake of interpreting perfectly normal feelings of discomfort as failure and give up prematurely. But big-vision small-enterprise owners who have been in business long enough to experience several cycles know that being expanded beyond your comfort zone is part of the terrain—and provides yet another opportunity for qualitative growth and mastery. "You never get comfortable with being uncomfortable. You just have to know that it's a phase you're going through at any given time," says Jessie Zapffe, proprietor of Golden Bough Books in Mount Shasta, California. "Discomfort isn't about failure, it's about growth and expansion. You're stepping out into new areas of your own capability, and that's not comfortable. But it's better than dying on the vine because a part of you isn't being used."

Think about your assumptions regarding success and failure as if the quality of your life, as you judge it at your end, depends on it. How often do you measure your success or failure against external, culturally defined standards instead of those that are aligned with your real lifestyle preferences, priorities, and needs? How can you know something or someone else is successful without being privy to the vision and goals of his business, for instance, or the heart, mind and happiness of the individual involved? The person whose apparent success you covet may be killing himself from the stress of pursuing goals that mean nothing to him, but that may never enter your mind. This is a critical flaw in our wonderfully abundant culture—to assume someone is successful and happy because they have specific tangible tokens of accomplishment; yet as outlined earlier, research shows that pursuing and owning these things doesn't in itself deliver happiness or meaning and can actually increase depression and an inability to sustain relationships.[14]

Is a quantitative definition of success truly success if it ultimately leaves you sick, lonely, dissatisfied, or unfulfilled? In the development of your big-vision small enterprise, reflect on and create your own definition of success, so the standards that you set and the actions that you take in striving toward and accomplishing it are rewarding and meaningful.

Chapter 22

TIME AND BALANCE

MANY BUSINESS OWNERS with whom I spoke and many managers and leaders with whom I've consulted mention a perceived lack of time as their key challenge. Given that everyone on the planet has the same amount of time available to him or her, our perceptions of time deficit aren't about time itself but about how we use it. So what does that make the issues of time and balance? For the big-vision small-business owner, they're opportunities for developing mastery and sharpening yet another qualitative growth edge.

Business owners, like many other people, seem to have an overwhelming number of issues and responsibilities competing for their attention on any given day. And many of them seem pretty disorganized, which affects every-thing from punctuality to how quickly they respond to phone calls or e-mail messages (if they have a system that helps manage such communications at all!). With such a long to-do list, it's no wonder that time seems to evaporate. How is it, then, that some individuals seem to accomplish so much more than others?

As philosopher Jacob Needleman writes in his book *Time and the Soul,* "It is only the Self that overcomes time." And the rewards of Self-revealing, big-vision practices are tangible. Needleman follows with an astute insight about the inherent conflict between having an obsession with time and wanting to nurture the Voice of the Self that makes the need for time management moot.[15]

There can be an uncomfortable tension between, on one hand, the psychological reality that being obsessed with time (or the lack of it) distances you from a so-called time-management solution and, on the other hand, the practical reality that there is much among your daily responsibilities that calls for your attention. While philosophical writings can help you find a more balanced perspective regarding time and how you approach it, you still live in a world where time measures and constraints are given importance.

In the real, versus idyllic, world, there are issues that, if not deftly approached, contribute to the perception of "not having enough time"; these include delegation, time management, deadline acceleration, "time cramps" created by resistance to necessary action, and a feeling of having the way you spend your time being out of balance with your priorities (or at least what you think your priorities *should* be). A good solution for me is to partner philosophical or spiritual practices with the more practical time-management strategies. For example, prioritizing my daily task list makes an enormous difference in the pace of the day, while meditation helps foster the clarity that can allow me to see what my real priorities are and find time where I thought none existed.

Some business owners have other time-management difficulties. When I first started interviewing business owners for this book, for example, several entrepreneurs expressed genuine interest in participating but missed several telephone interview appointments because of poor time management and delegation abilities. Their tendency is probably to "fire fight," or jump from crisis to crisis, and thus they're never in control of how they spend their workday. Sound familiar?

Crisis junkies may be addicted to the adrenalin rush of being in crisis mode and refrain from delegating to others on their team who are either qualified to assist or who could develop the skills necessary to manage some, if not all, of the details currently hoarded by the business owner. To that, you might say, "I don't *have* anyone on my team who can do this." Maybe so, but there are likely employees who could take on additional responsibilities and, in doing so, clear out some of the clutter from your day. Without giving them an opportunity, these individuals will never develop the facility to manage such responsibilities with confidence—their own and yours. If your team is truly stretched to capacity and you and others are still fire fighting throughout the day, you need to review whether disorganization or inefficiency are problems or whether your staffing and revenue plans need to be revisited. These are symptoms that often respond well to big-vision medicine, and that's one prescription you can write yourself.

Additional time-related bad habits include chronically accelerating your deadlines (a syndrome I battle) and giving yourself "time cramps" by resisting action when you know action is needed. Accelerating your deadlines—starting with a realistic deadline and then immediately moving your due dates closer—makes you anxious for at least two reasons: the new deadlines are inevitably unrealistic and add unnecessary activities to your daily to-do list. This exacerbates your short-term time crunch. Isn't it amazing that you cause yourself such suffering? Fortunately, skills in prioritization, efficiency, time and personal management, and clear thinking are, if not inherent, learnable. And once again, the big-vision small-business owner sees such deficits as opportunities for cultivating mastery, gaining wisdom, and using both to better serve his organization's stakeholders—employees, customers, vendors, and others in the community beyond.

There is a potentially high cost of not choosing some strategy, of allowing imbalance to be your default. "One of the problems is that, as business owners, we spend so many hours in our businesses that we give up all of our hobbies, some of our friends, and our lives," says Bill Hayes of Estey Printing in Boulder, Colorado. "The focus, particularly for men, is growing the business and securing our future. Because of that, a lot of men who own businesses also go through divorce." Hayes found himself feeling burned out in 1998 and took a three-month sabbatical to determine if he wanted to continue being a business owner. Although he seriously considered selling his business, he ultimately decided to buy another firm. As a result, he doubled the size of his business and added a seasoned operations manager who was adept at managing the printing firm's staff—something Hayes had previously done.

"During my three months off, I planted 300 bulbs in my garden," remembers Hayes. "There has to be a balance between family, your employees, and yourself. Don't give up your hobbies; don't give up your family; don't work every single day. Go home and garden, because you can't grow your business if you're not having a good home life."

As with everything else, what constitutes balance is subjective. "Balance to me is having everything in my life that I want," said Linda Manassee Buell, founder and owner of Simplify Life in Poway, California. "That means having time for myself, for my family and for my business." Buell spent 17 years as a corporate manager before starting her own company to share what she learned in her quest for a more balanced life. "When you're doing the things you love in your life and having the things you love in your life, and you're saying 'yes' to the things you love, life is simple," said Buell. "When it's not that way, we're saying 'yes' to things we don't really want to say 'yes' to."

When Buell begins working with a client who is searching for more meaning and balance in his life, she asks him to create a vision of what he wants his life to look like. If he's like many people, the client might have difficulty with this task and find it easier to begin by identifying the pieces of his current reality that he'd like to see changed. Another question that Buell might ask her client is "What behavior are you modeling to your children, employees, or clients," and then he should determine whether that would be a part of the optimal vision. Once the client has defined what a more balanced life would look like for him, Buell will often ask him to become disciplined in using a daily planner to list out all of the key priorities and activities for the upcoming week and each day, including personal and family activities. She recommends assigning a color code for key categories of activity—self, family, business, community, and so forth—to make it easier to see where imbalance might be lurking and priorities are skewed. While such an assignment seems simple enough, and is certainly valuable, some of her clients find the shift grueling.

"Some people just aren't used to operating on a self-directing basis," she said. "If they're coming from a corporate background, they're used to working at someone else's direction. They might be used to operating off deadlines and like that adrenaline rush. It's like an addiction, so in changing that, they're operating in a way that feels different at first. Ultimately, they get to the point where operating under that crisis-inspired adrenaline rush just doesn't feel right."

Just as with an addiction, changing the behavioral habits that create imbalance can be challenging, so that guiding vision is crucial. "Vision is very important, whether that's the big vision for your business, the vision for your life with your family, or even your vision for what your house or office look like when they're cleaned up," emphasized Buell. "That vision will help you focus when you're in the tunnel and things look hard and painful. The vision is what will help you move through that pain and fear."[16]

What does "living in balance" mean to you? What are your highest priorities? Does the way you currently spend your time reflect these priorities? If not, look at how you can reprioritize, delegate, or better manage your time so that you're attending to the people, activities, and things that really *are* important to you. Don't wait until you have time, because by then you may have to pay an unpleasant price. Do it sooner rather than later and make sure you're living according to your highest priorities. What can help you find the clarity and inspiration to pursue this and other big-vision priorities? Choosing a slate of wisdom and mastery practices that is appropriate to your spiritual or philosophical tradition and lifestyle. The next chapter offers ideas and reflections on some of the options that are available to you.

Chapter 23

WISDOM AND MASTERY PRACTICES

IN HIS BOOK *Spirit Matters*, Rabbi Michael Lerner writes that each of us has an opportunity "to bring forward as much consciousness, love, solidarity, creativity, sensitivity, and goodness as we possibly can."[17] Though Rabbi Lerner is not talking specifically to big-vision small-business owners, he could very well be.

The primary purpose of cultivating a faith or mastery practice is to keep your focus and actions closer to such virtues and further away from a mentality of scarcity instead of abundance, competition without collaboration, and callousness instead of kindness. These are some of the very virtues that lead a small business into the big-vision realm of mastery. All lofty ideals, no doubt, but recent scientific research shows practicality in this brand of idealism, whether linking prayer with healing, meditation with lower blood pressure, or pink jailhouse walls with fewer incidents of violence.[18]

The intangible practice can yield distinctly tangible outcomes. Be your own scientific experiment. If you've already cultivated a wisdom or mastery practice, review it, refine it, and recommit yourself. If you don't have such a practice (be honest!), identify several options from the list below or from other resources and create a one-month calendar for your new practice. Make it a priority for at least 15 minutes a day for no less than a one-month period. The results will give you ample cause to continue, and help you find the inspiration and insight that nourishes your big-vision ideals into reality.

There are many books, organizations, and Web-site resources with information about the wide variety of wisdom and mastery practices available to you. What follows are some reflections on the activities from my own repertoire, from which I draw for my personal faith and mindset practice. I don't do all of these things every day but, across the span of any given month, I endeavor to do some combination of these activities or disciplines regularly.

The result? For me, greater clarity, less time feeling scattered, more awareness of how my mind plays tricks on me, a feeling of connection to others, and a decreased likelihood that I jump to conclusions or fall prey to someone who's trying (purposely or not) to push my hot buttons. In general, when I'm minding my faith practice, I feel more connected to a Source that is much wiser and stronger than I am alone, which gives me a great sense of well-being and helps me make better decisions, regardless of the day's chaos. When I'm not finding time for my practice, the results are quite the opposite. Here are a few options for your big-vision toolbox:

Personal Reflections on Mastery and Wisdom Practice

Allowing versus forcing. If you're a control freak, I feel your pain and know firsthand that this practice offers both significant challenge and significant reward. Assuming you own a business or feel competent enough to give business ownership a go, I would guess that you're fairly (if not especially) skilled in finding your way from blank canvas to finished painting and have a specific vision of how exactly that might happen. That means you like to have a certain amount of control over the circumstances, and perhaps people and resources, to get things done.

Yet there are times (almost always) when trying to control every factor relevant to a particular goal or need is like trying to sweep water up a hill. And what happens then? Instead of adopting a realistic perspective—that sweeping water uphill is a losing proposition—you try and try until you become stressed and fatigued by your inability to control the circumstances you deem crucial to your vision and well-being. What is the reality? That very little is actually in your control. As the ancient Stoic philosophers knew, wise men and women that they were, the only thing you can truly control is your own thinking and behavior. Everything else, from the weather to the stock market to someone else's behavior, including his or her love for or rejection of you, is well beyond your control. And coming to that understanding can be intensely liberating.

In deciding to mind your own thoughts and behavior—or "show up to the party," as a friend of mine puts it—you can then practice your ability to allow factors outside of your control to find their own order within the seeming chaos, or to rightfully fall to the wayside as truly unimportant to your well-being. Sounds tough, doesn't it? It can be, primarily because it's impossible for many of us to believe that such an order will arrive unforced. We lack faith, whether in our own ability or the presence of our guiding force. One way to overcome this doubt is to see the concept of "allowing" not as a matter of being passive, because that would be a misperception,

"Faith is a mental attitude that is so convinced of its own idea—which so completely accepts it—that any contradiction is unthinkable and impossible."

ERNEST HOLMES

but more as a matter of doing what's within your control and then trusting your ability to adapt or respond to other circumstances that come your way. You can, in the spirit of the Tao Te Ching, be like the valley through which the rivers flow.

Communication skillfulness. Interpersonal and organizational communication is an area of professional focus for me, and yet communication can also be a sacred practice in and of itself. Most wisdom traditions focus not on our separation from others but on our connection to others. What's more, faith teachings emphasize the quality of our interactions and interconnections, whether called right relationship or doing unto others as we would have them do unto us. Communication skillfulness—your ability to listen deeply or speak clearly and compassionately—requires that you align your heart and mind with the more technical skills of interpersonal communication. That means you watch your intentions, unclutter your mind, and focus completely on someone else for a period of time, as might be the case in a meeting or for a more fleeting connection, as on the bus or in a grocery store line.

To communicate well is to commune with others, build stronger relationships, and feel the satisfaction inherent in deeper connections. Right communication is not specific to any one faith or mastery tradition but a primary component of right relationship and thus a big-vision small-business area of opportunity. You can practice skillful communication throughout your normal workday and after (although you can also schedule times to practice more deeply). Section Three explores the key big-vision practice of right relationship and communication in greater depth.

Nature. My parents trained me early to see breathing fresh air and communing with nature as a source of relaxation and inspiration. My mother was forever encouraging my sisters and me to "Turn off that television and go outside." My father, who in addition to being a fellow introvert is a renowned conservation and outdoors enthusiast, took me along on fishing trips and hiking expeditions around his camp in the country. The lesson stuck: when I need to clear my mind or unclog my inspiration channels, I head outdoors, whether for a walk around the block or a trip up the coast or to the mountains.

Aside from exercise and clarifying doses of fresh air and sunshine—which are benefits not to be underestimated—getting out into nature offers valuable life and business lessons. When I take a walk or go for a hike, everywhere I turn I see evidence of the natural cycle of life. Whether in the city or country, some things are just sprouting, some are nearing the end of their life cycle, and others have long since died. Some plants are vibrant in color, while others are more subdued. Tides ebb and flow, and rivers and streams rush toward the sea or trickle to a near stop. Creatures emerge ravenous from a period of hibernation or gather resources in anticipation of leaner times. Winter, like the desert, seems cruel and stark, yet both teem with creation and life. Nature reminds me that "for everything there is a season, a reason for everything under the sun." Far from being impractical, these lessons are directly applicable to the cycles that occur, like it or not, in business.

Gratitude. Gratitude seems like something you have, not something you practice. But practicing gratitude can have a profound effect on the quality of your day and thus, as a practice, enrich your life. By choosing to spend some portion of your day focusing on those things for which you're grateful, you spend that much less time stewing over what you don't have or what didn't happen. Given that many people, based on a multitude of philosophical and faith traditions, believe that you attract into your life that which you spend significant time thinking about, watching what you think about makes sense.

Yet practicing gratitude, particularly if you're openly doing so, can be more difficult than it should be. This reality, particularly in our culture, fascinates me. How often have you heard, for example, people apologize for seeming "Pollyanna-ish" due to their optimism or positive thinking? How sick are we as a culture that we feel sheepish when we're not steeped in pessimism, negativity, or feelings of victimization? You'd be surprised at how often you encounter resistance after you speak openly in the language of gratitude, when what you hear back from others is a litany of "Yeah, but . . ." and "Well it's easy for you, but . . ." But, but, but. So practicing gratitude can be unnerving for others, particularly if it marks a change from an old habit of more negative, scarcity-based thinking. As massage therapist Christopher Adamo said, "We commiserate in misery, but we hoard our joy." Big-vision business owners choose not to wallow in misery but to share both their abundance and their joy.

> *"You who are the*
> *source of all power*
> *Whose rays illumi-*
> *nate the whole world*
> *Illuminate also*
> *my heart*
> *So that it too can*
> *do your work."*
> BOOK OF RUNES

Many of the business owners with whom I spoke for this book said they felt lucky to own a business or blessed because the road rose up to meet them time and again. A gratitude practice promotes such an overall feeling of abundance. You can spend five minutes in the morning listing three things for which you're grateful in that moment, or you can focus a daily prayer or meditation on the concept or feeling of gratitude. Regardless, the reminder of the many ways in which you're blessed, of the many things for which you can feel gratitude, can lend buoyancy during times of challenge and momentum from the realization that you're always in a season of plenty should you choose to see it.

Prayer and meditation. If I had to select one practice that is the most important to my sense of equilibrium and well-being, I'd have to choose prayer and meditation. These are what I would call Source practices, from which all others can flow. What's the difference between prayer and meditation? One of the best definitions I've seen is that prayer is when you talk to God or highest wisdom, and meditation is when you listen for the response. A balanced practice makes time for both.

Occasionally I'm asked, in true Californian fashion, what type of prayer and meditation I practice. Asking such a thing in casual conversation would have been considered rude in the Northeast, where I grew up. The question both amuses and frustrates me, primarily because the person asking almost always believes that there is only one way to do each. But that's not so. The variety of ways we can pray and meditate is in itself a miracle and an inspiration.

Beyond that initial definition of talking to God and listening for a response, prayer and meditation can take many forms other than the most obvious or familiar. You can create a space and assign a specific time for daily prayer; read sacred texts and reflect on their meaning in your daily life; sit in prayer or meditation; make certain activities a kind of prayer or meditation, as Mohandas Gandhi did with his spinning; or do walking prayer or meditation. You might, as the Zen practitioners do, center your attention on your breathing. Or you may choose centering prayer, in which you repeat a sacred word or favorite prayer or center your mind on a virtue such as generosity or love.

Living in San Francisco, I'm most fortunate to be surrounded by people taking a variety of paths to Truth. Walking in my neighborhood, I see or hear Buddhism, the Tao, Confucianism, Judaism, Catholicism, Christian Orthodoxy, Protestantism, New Age, Christian Science, Mormonism, Islam, Hinduism, and other belief systems in action. I smell the incense and see the prayer shrines and each time am reminded of how important it is to make a place for the sacred among my daily activities.

Service to others. Would it change your day if upon waking you asked, "How can I be of service?" If, after asking, you journeyed through your day as if each circumstance provided an answer to your question? Just as each of these practices helps to rejuvenate us and generate inspiration so do they offer an opportunity for mastery that can ultimately benefit our employees, customers, and others who are affected by our big-vision enterprise.

I have several favorite anecdotes or readings to help remind me of the practice of service to others. One is attributed to Mother Teresa who, upon being asked how one could change the world, responded with her trademark directness, "If you want to change the world, pick up a broom." Like Dorothy Day, another proponent of the value of "the little work," Mother Teresa reminds us that great change and great contribution finds itself in our willingness to do the small things—picking up a broom, answering the phone, doing paperwork—with an attitude of service and generosity.

> *"It is high time the idea of success should be replaced with the ideal of service."*
>
> ALBERT EINSTEIN

In *The Seven Spiritual Laws of Success*, Dr. Deepak Chopra also suggests that being of service doesn't have to be expensive or elaborate. You can be of service in the smallest of ways, such as holding open a door, offering a seat on a bus, or giving a smile to someone who might treasure that contact in an otherwise lonely day. Chopra writes, "When you meet someone, you can silently send them a blessing, wishing them happiness, joy and laughter."[19]

Most mornings as I ready myself to begin my workday, I reflect on one of several prayers, such as that of St. Francis of Assisi. The Assisi prayer orients me toward being of service to others instead of solely to myself. When I say, "Make me an instrument of your peace" or "Grant not that I seek to be consoled, but to console others; to be understood but to understand others; to be loved but to love others," I shift into an awareness that, instead of being self-centered and brusque, I can serve through my willingness to listen or in a humble offering of even the smallest gesture of compassion or kindness.

Mindfulness. *Mindfulness* is a word that is often associated with Buddhism. However, the concept of mindfulness also appears in other practices, both sacred and philosophical. Many traditions urge us to wake up and be conscious to what we're doing at any given moment. Mindfulness—or awareness—is a matter of paying attention, right now. Think about how often you're doing one thing—meeting with someone, for instance—but you're really not there at all. Instead, you're thinking about something that happened yesterday or how something will work out tomorrow. You're preoccupied with something other than the person with whom you're meeting.

You might also walk, eat, or even drive mindlessly and find yourself tripping or bumping into things, choking on or spilling your food, or driving into the back of someone else's car. Lama Surya Das, teacher and author of *Awakening the Buddha Within*, wrote, "Our lack of mindfulness makes us careless: Often we hurt others without thinking or sometimes even without noticing we've done so."[20]

If you're preoccupied or careless, you're missing an opportunity to hone and demonstrate the big-vision practices that can distinguish a small enterprise. As with many spiritual practices, nurturing a habit of being more aware has very tangible results—results that are aligned with big-vision priorities. "I'm much more conscious of trying to deal with things as they are rather than how I want them to be. I'm more in tune with reality, versus what I think or would want to happen," says Susan Griffin-Black, founder of EO Products in Corte Madera, California. Griffin-Black has seen her business through a number of typical challenges, including buying out her original investors, regulating cash flows, and presiding over an expanding number of retail outlets. She has seen practical benefits in her approach toward her business since beginning a meditation and mindfulness practice nearly a decade ago:

> *"Paperwork, cleaning the house, dealing with the innumerable visitors who come all through the day, answering the phone, keeping patience and acting intelligently, which is to find some meaning in all that happens—these things, too, are the works of peace."*
>
> DOROTHY DAY, THE CATHOLIC WORKER

Everyone has two modes of behavior: times when you're paying attention to what's happening in the moment, and times when you're on automatic. When you're on automatic, behaving as you think you should, the possibility for being reactive is higher. When you're more mindful, the possibility of being calm, kind, and thoughtful is heightened. You make better decisions for the long term, versus when you are reacting and are more apt to lose your temper and make foolish decisions.

When you are mindful, you're making a decision to pay attention to what you're doing, as you're doing it. You become more aware. For example, you might notice things you've not seen before even though you drive past them every day, or you'll observe yourself reacting to certain situations or personalities in an unproductive way. Or you'll make different decisions about what you choose to say to someone else, because you're more aware of how your words affect others.

Just try it. Make a commitment to being more aware today, and you'll notice how often you're simply not paying attention. And then you'll see a field of opportunities for qualitative growth and mastery within your organization.

Journaling.   Journals have been the tool of choice for dreamers, explorers, and movement leaders. In the past, people could save the letters received from friends and loved ones, and the letters themselves became a type of journal. But today, in the faster and more crammed world that technology has allowed, people must make a more deliberate decision to write about their experiences, challenges, and insights in a journal.

Aside from being a chronicle of your big-vision journey, as so many journals in hindsight become, taking pen in hand to write in a notebook can produce an unexpected bonus. The very act of writing by hand forces you to slow your thoughts and quiet the incessant chatter that is the hallmark of the busy mind. Liken it to driving: Imagine that you have an appointment with a wise counselor and are looking for a particular address in an unfamiliar place. Are you more likely to find what you're looking for if you're speeding along at 75 miles per hour, or if you slow down to a speed that allows distinctive buildings and signs to emerge from the blur of what you're passing?

There are other journaling exercises that can be helpful in solving a problem or seeing a situation differently. One that you might find interesting involves writing out a question or issue in your nondominant hand.[21] What's the point? As Albert Einstein said, you won't solve problems by using the same approach that got you where you are to begin with. When you do something differently, such as writing with your left hand if you usually use your right, you break a pattern. In the process, you might allow yourself a more creative way of seeing or thinking.

You can also draw, use crayons or other colored writing tools, or glue in words or pictures you've cut from a magazine. You might be thinking, "I don't have time for that. Besides, that's for children." What do you think it means that, to reach the kingdom of heaven, you must become like a child again? Many creative activities seem childish, and yet creativity awakens inspiration. And inspiration is exactly what you need to fuel your enthusiasm and meet the challenges of business ownership in unusual and energizing ways. So if your inner adult is really that oppressive, schedule a date with a child to journal, color, and make a collage. Better yet, designate a big-vision collage day where you and your group can reflect on strengths and dream up new opportunities to hone gifts and share them with the world.

Wellness and rejuvenation. I have a confession to make. One of the excuses I loathe most is "I just don't have the time." I just flat out don't believe that's true. In fact, as excuses go, I think this one is lame and uncreative. How often do you say this? Make a promise to yourself, right now, that you'll no longer use this excuse. You have as much time as everyone else on the planet. How you spend that time is your choice, so you choose not to do something. Big-vision small-business owners know that you can't pursue high ideals if you're feeling fatigued or burned out.

Why does this come up in a section about wellness and rejuvenation? Because many people claim not to have the time for activities that will renew them, and then complain about how exhausted they are. Maybe you've said this yourself. Do you say you're too busy to eat a decent lunch in a civil time frame that doesn't require you to choke down your food? Do you complain about your aching back, shoulders, neck, or arms but say you're too busy to schedule an appointment with a neuromuscular massage professional? Do you lament the degree to which your business has taken over your life while insisting that you don't have the time to see a movie, read a nonbusiness book, or go to the park? Can you see that an alternative is just one decision away?

Attending to your wellness is another source practice that, if tended carefully, allows you to fulfill your obligations more healthfully and skillfully. When you make sure your mind, body, and spirit are well fed, you become less tired, harried, scattered, and reactive. You find that you do, indeed, have the time for everything that's most important to you, including your wellness practice. Taking care of yourself might mean eating healthfully (and not rushing through your meals); getting physical exercise, whether taking a short walk or running a marathon; spending time in prayer or meditation to quiet your mind and ease your physical and mental stress; playing with children or animal companions; nurturing a hobby; scheduling a regular appointment at a spa; or any number of other activities that suit your interests and are therefore things you'll do regularly.

Support from advisers and peers. Cultivating a support network is such a worthwhile practice that I'm always amazed when a business owner, for whatever reason, refuses to seek counsel and wisdom from others. I often come across individuals who feel the enormous pressures of business ownership but who refuse to identify peers from whom they could seek guidance and ideas. According to Larisa Langley, who spent nearly five years with the San Antonio Chamber of Commerce before joining a small business herself, self-enforced isolation has a high price. "Some small-business owners can be very stubborn, and that can be a very good thing. They're not going to give up," says Langley. "But that stubbornness can be their downfall because they're incapable of asking for help or asking for assistance when they need to."

Tricia Keener Blaha, owner of Green House, Inc., in Boise, Idaho, is of Okee and Cherokee ancestry and is committed to regularly incorporating both Native American rituals and feedback from people outside of her business into her daily routine. Blaha believes it's important that her informal advisory board feature diverse perspectives, including those of her financial consultant, a brother-in-law who is an attorney, and a Cherokee medicine woman who is both a business owner and a spiritual adviser. "You can love your work, but your work can't love you back," says Blaha. "Every day, you put all that energy out into the business. You have to have that outer circle to fill back up again. I have a circle and teachers who support me and care about me for me, not just because of what I do in my business."

A business owner's circle might include peers with whom you meet over lunch or coffee (or even via e-mail); an informal advisory board made up of your attorney, accountant, and another business owner or two; or a mentor who has been in business longer than you. There are an increasing number of associations for independently owned small businesses and conscious or socially responsible enterprises. You can also hire a personal coach to provide regular counsel, a person who will demand accountability from you as you undertake the journey from living according to someone else's standards to the more authentic reality and balance you've envisioned. Since isolation can be very narrowing, a big-vision small-business owner can find both support and inspiration for the journey by cultivating relationships with like-spirited colleagues.

Baseball. This list wouldn't be complete for me without baseball, which may seem an unlikely candidate for a wisdom and mastery practice list. But any baseball lover will understand why it's included here. To me, as to other lovers of the diamond sport, baseball is a great metaphor for life and offers many important reminders to those whose game of choice is putting together a mastery-level big-vision small enterprise. Endeavor to appreciate baseball, and many things become clear.

I followed the New York Yankees as a young girl growing up in upstate New York and then lost interest in the sport for more than a decade. When I tuned in to watch the Florida Marlins play the Cleveland Indians in the 1997 World Series, I became a baseball fan again. That was a great series, with long games played well beyond the usual nine innings. The players were putting everything they had on the line, out by out, inning by inning, game by game. The teams were well matched in skill, mindset, and heart, and winning a division, and certainly the series, requires all three. Therein you find the most important lessons.

Take the psychology of the closer, for example. For nonfans, the closer is the hard-throwing pitcher who finishes the game, usually coming out in the last inning to maintain the lead or prevent the other team from scoring. Three outs, a matter of minutes—that's all the time the closer has to do his job. When he's in flow and everything goes well, his team wins the game and he's a hero. If he has a bad night, which for a closer might amount to just one bad pitch, he makes his mistake in front of the 50,000 fans in attendance and thousands more watching the game on television. Instead of saving the win, his one mistake costs his team the game. As a result, the closer must be particularly adept at managing his mindset, staying in the moment, clearing out the noise, and relying on his experience and skill to do what's needed right then. After a bad night or even several horrendous outings, he must still come to the pitcher's mound thinking of nothing but what he has to pull off: Forget yesterday's loss and that he's been in a slump and do what it takes to get the next three batters out.

Similarly, a baseball player is cheered for his 0.334 batting average, which means that he's hit the ball one time out of every three chances, or failed two-thirds of the time. That 33 percent success ratio makes for a great year at the plate. Or a player might spend hours perfecting his mechanics—the smallest of details that most people don't notice but which make all the difference in the highest levels of performance. The great players and teams go further still. In the 2000 division playoffs, players interviewed before the game seemed uncertain and diffident. They and their team would inevitably lose the game that night. Individually and as a team, they weren't together in mind, body, and spirit. Watching them on the field, in contrast to other outings, they didn't seem altogether there. In their minds and hearts, they'd already lost the game. In a field where everyone is skilled, attending to mind and spirit—and doing it more often than not—becomes a distinguishing factor.

The same level of awareness, commitment, and mind-body-spirit integration is what allows a group of mastery-level athletes to knit themselves together into an effective team. The team might consist of high-achieving individuals, but it doesn't get to the playoffs or the World Series by remaining a team of self-absorbed soloists. Each player is responsible not only for his own skillfulness and mindset management but also for staying focused on and conscious of what everyone else is doing at any given point during a game or season. It's rare to hear the real champions—those who are leaders in the clubhouse as well as on the field—whine about harsh circumstances or poor outings. And that's what separates them from average athletes, just as higher levels of commitment and higher standards or ideals distinguish a big-vision small-enterprise owner from the crowd.

The game of baseball is full of such lessons, of examples of peak-performance psychology and of the cyclical nature of things. And many people find the same lessons, or just relaxation, in their sport of choice, be it golf, football, soccer, hockey, or professional wrestling. But from April through October, you can be certain that I'm making the time to watch the San Francisco Giants, regardless of how busy the day looks. I'm always amazed at how it parallels my life and how its lessons can be easily adapted when I head into the office the day after a great game.

Parting Thoughts

Where Do You Go from Here?

Among the many pearls of wisdom that he shared, Mohandas Gandhi reminded us that "the path is the goal." The same is true for the big-vision small business, where the journey offers the opportunity to pursue and practice high ideals, do something worthwhile, and become a perpetual learner who has created an organization of learners. The road, which falls somewhere between small business and fast-growth or large corporate organizations, can seem a lonely, self-punishing one at times. This, despite our genuine beliefs that it is the journey that matters and that a socially conscious vision or mission is well worth the difficulties that arise along the way.

For this reason, making the choice to pursue qualitative growth as a big-vision small enterprise, instead of following the more traditional fast-growth model, requires a business owner to be confident, self-secure, and committed as well as visionary. Yet we may find comfort in numbers, thanks to a growing movement underway—one with several tributaries—that lends support and encouragement to those of us who are opting to develop human-scale, spiritually or socially conscious enterprises whose motives and priorities are something different than the "grow big at any human cost" norm.

There are communities of people who are uniting to revitalize or create dynamic Main Streets by encouraging small enterprise and local self-sufficiency, and those who are rallying together to generate awareness and support of independently owned, community-accountable small businesses. There are those within the movement to promote socially responsible business who favor smaller, human-scale enterprises over colossal corporations. There are others who believe that small businesses are crucial participants in the campaign for better environmental stewardship, primarily because of the sheer number of small businesses that exist and the fact that they leave a smaller footprint. And then there are the enterprise owners whose spiritual or philosophical traditions lead them to practice in and serve by creating smaller, socially and spiritually conscious businesses. While there isn't one association or network that connects all of these communities, their very existence offers big-vision small-business owners the potential for inspiration and connection.

In addition to seeking out other small-enterprise owners who are not just likeminded but like-spirited as well, you can apply the tenets shared in this book with peers within your own localities or associations. You can engage others in dynamic discussions about the possibilities stemming from big-vision principles. And you can unite your staff members (or collaboration partners) in dialogue about your own organization's big-vision characteristics, gifts, and priorities. Using the big-vision priorities, golden rules, bibliography, and the many dialogue starters and questions offered in this book, you can identify your organizational strengths and opportunities to seek a higher level of mastery in the way you do business. By doing so, you will radiate the big-vision small business "essence" through each interaction, thus becoming a beacon or inspiration to others for what is possible.

> *"If you're going to sweep the floor, sweep it better than anybody in town."*
>
> CARLOS SANTANA

Though an organizational leader can certainly choose to grow the company quantitatively in keeping with the more traditional models, this book has offered the suggestion that there are other pathways to growth. You can find success and satisfaction without expanding your payroll, square footage, revenue base, or number of locations. Small enterprise can be rewarding in itself and offers a much greater potential for another type of growth and contribution—one of quality rather than quantity—that has been too long overlooked in our zeal for chasing the big numbers.

Creating a big-vision small business is such a possibility, and an open-ended one at that. As a big-vision small-enterprise owner, you define the standards of mastery you will strive toward and engage with your employees, vendors, or collaboration partners to put that vision into action.

Again, we think of Lao Tzu's gentle reminder: The journey of a thousand miles begins with one step. The best place to start is right where you are. I hope this book provides one valuable and inspiring resource for you as you define the fuller potential that your enterprise holds.

Wishing you well on your journey!

 *Notes*

INTRODUCTION: THE GREAT POWER OF SMALL ENTERPRISE

1. Portrait of Small Business USA, November 2001 (a study conducted by Bigstep and Working Solo, Inc.).

SECTION ONE
KEY NO. 1: THERE'S MORE THAN ONE WAY TO DEFINE GROWTH

1. Susan Greco, "I Was Seduced by the New Economy," *Inc. Magazine*, February 1999, p. 34.

2. U.S. Small Business Administration, Washington, D.C., December 2000 (www.sbaonline.sba.gov).

3. Working Solo, Inc. (www.workingsolo.com).

4. Europa—European Commission, "Definition of Small and Medium Sized Enterprises" (http://europa.eu.int/comm/enterprise/consultations/sme_definition/).

5. U.S. Census Bureau, "Statistics About Business Size" (http://www.census.gov/epcd/www/smallbus.html).

6. U.S. Small Business Administration Office of Advocacy, "State of Small Business Report," 1998.

7. National Small Business United, "Small Business Statistics," Washington, D.C., December 2000 (www.nsbu.org); Seattle Chamber of Commerce, "National Small Business Statistics," Seattle, WA, December 2000 (www.seattlechamber.com); U.S. Small Business Administration, "Small Business Vital Statistics," Washington, D.C., December 2000 (www.sbaonline.sba.gov); Working Solo, Inc., "SOHO Statistics" (www.workingsolo.com); TheManager.org, "Small Business—Size as a Chance or Handicap" (www.themanager.org).

8. U.S. Small Business Administration study conducted by University of Oregon professor of accounting Pat Frishkoff.

9. Alex Salkever, "Special Report: The Future of Apple," *BusinessWeek Online*; January 18, 2002 (www.businessweek.com).

10. Sarah van Gelder, in dialogue with David Korten and Paul Hawken, "Corporate Futures," *Yes! A Journal of Positive Futures*, Summer 1999 (www.futurenet.org).

11. Craig Savoye, "Vanilla Suburbs Seek an Identity: Small 'Edge Cities' Are Building Downtowns in a Brick-and-Mortar Quest for a Sense of Community and Character," *Christian Science Monitor*, December 30, 1999, pp. 1–3 (www.csmonitor.com).

12. Stewart L. Tubbs, *A Systems Approach to Small Group Interaction*, 4th ed. (McGraw-Hill, 1992), pp. 104–105.

13. Dagmar Recklies, "Small Business—Size as a Chance or Handicap," TheManager.org, March 10, 2001 (www.themanager.org); Hon. Ahmad Kamal, Pakistani Ambassador to the United Nations and professor, New York University, International Studies: Lesson 9: Role of the Private Sector and Civil Society (http://www.nyu.edu/wagner/international/kamal/kamalnotes_lesson9.htm).

14. Noel Tichy, "The Growth Imperative," *Leader to Leader*, no. 14, Fall 1999, p. 24.

15. Larry Greiner, "Evolution and Revolution as Organizations Grow," *Harvard Business Review*, July–August 1972 (reprint no. 72407).

16. Paul Geroski, "The Corporate Growth Puzzle," *The Economist*, July 17, 1999, p. 70.

17. John Peterman, "The Rise and Fall of the J. Peterman Company," *Harvard Business Review*, September–October 1999, pp. 59–66 (reprint no. 99507); Greco, "I Was Seduced by the New Economy," p. 57; Shira J. Boss, "A Cowboy Clothier Mounts a Comeback," *Christian Science Monitor*, December 11, 2000.

SECTION TWO
KEY NO. 2: TO LIVE LARGE,
YOU HAVE TO VISION BIG

1. Carol, Adrienne, *The Purpose of Your Life* (New York: Eagle Brook/William Morrow, 1998), p. 158.

2. JoAnn Dahlkoetter, "Realizing Your Potential," *Your Performing Edge* (San Carlos, CA, 1996), www.yourperformingedge.com.

3. Daniel Denison and Caroline Fisher, "Why Mission Matters," *Leader to Leader*, no. 17 (Summer 2000), p. 46.

4. Bob Metcalfe, "The Visionary Thing," *Wired* 7, no. 11 (November 1999), pp. 300–303.

5. Tom Johnson and Alan White, "Six Principles of Business in the 21st Century," *Civilization*, February 2000, p. 61 (www.civmag.com).

6. Craig Savoye, "Workers Say Honesty Is Best Company Policy," *Christian Science*

Monitor, June 15, 2000, p. 3; Del Jones, "Doing the Wrong Thing: 48% of Workers Admit to Unethical or Illegal Acts," *USA Today*, April 4, 1997, p. A-1.

7. Waddock, Sandra; "Fluff Is Not Enough: Managing Responsibility for Corporate Citizenship," *Ethical Corporation Magazine*, February 22, 2002.

8. "Business Ethics: Doing Well by Doing Good," *The Economist*, April 22, 2000, pp. 65–67.

9. *Webster's College Dictionary* (New York: Random House, 1996).

10. Linda Ellinor and Glenna Gerard, *Dialogue: Rediscover the Transforming Power of Conversation* (New York: John Wiley & Sons, 1998), p. 3; William Isaacs, *Dialogue and the Art of Thinking Together* (New York: Currency/Doubleday, 1999); Daniel Yankelovich, *The Magic of Dialogue: Transforming Conflict into Cooperation* (New York: Simon & Schuster, 1999).

11. Ivy Sea Online, Ivy Sea, Inc., San Francisco, CA (www.ivysea.com).

12. David Cooperrider et al., *Appreciative Inquiry* (Champaign, IL: Stipes Publishing, 1999).

SECTION THREE
KEY NO. 3: RIGHT RELATIONSHIP IS A BIG-VISION CRAFT

1. Foundation for Community Encouragement, *FCE Communiqué*, Summer 2000, p. 11. For the story of *The Rabbi's Gift*, see M. Scott Peck, *The Different Drum: Community Making and Peace* (New York: Simon & Schuster, 1987), pp. 13–15; or www.catholicvocation.org.au/cv_rabbbigift.htm.

2. Rebecca Z. Shafir, *The Zen of Listening: Mindful Communication in the Age of Distraction* (Wheaton, IL: Quest Books, 2000). Marshall Rosenberg, *Nonviolent Communication: A Language of Compassion* (Del Mar, CA: PuddleDancer Press, 1999).

3. American Society for Training & Development, *Training & Development*, December 1998, p. 13 (www.astd.org).

4. *Manager's Legal Bulletin*; September 2000.

5. Alfie Kohn, "Challenging Behaviorist Dogma: Myths about Money and Motivation," *Compensation and Benefits Review*, March/April 1998; Kohn, "For Best Results, Forget the Bonus," *New York Times*; October 17, 1993; and www.alfiekohn.org/

6. Alfie Kohn, *No Contest: The Case against Competition* (New York: Houghton Mifflin, 1986, 1992); www.alfiekohn.org/

7. Carolyn Said, "Dot-Com Escape," *San Francisco Chronicle*, September 18, 2000; www.sfgate.com/

8. Tom Johnson and Alan White, "Six Principles of Business in the 21st Century," *Civilization*, February 2000, p. 61; www.civmag.com/

9. For more on corporate jargon, see www.buzzkiller.net/

10. For resources regarding leadership and organizational communication, see Ivy Sea

Online, www.ivysea.com/

11. "Entrepreneurs are Deluded: Official," *The Economist*, July 17, 1997.

12. Dawn Rivers Baker, *Wahmpreneur News Magazine* 3, no. 25, February 18, 2002; www.wahmpreneur.com/

SECTION FOUR
KEY NO. 4: TO LIVE FROM THE SOURCE, REPLENISH THE WELL

1. Matthew Fox, *The Reinvention of Work: A New Vision of Livelihood for Our Time* (New York: HarperCollins, 1994), p. 5.

2. Mark Forstater, *The Spiritual Teachings of Marcus Aurelius* (New York: Harper-Collins, 2000); Maxwell Staniforth, *Marcus Aurelius Meditations* (New York: Penguin Classics, 1964).

3. European Baha'i Business Forum, "Mission and Core Beliefs of EBBF" (Chambéry, France); Bryan Graham, "The Baha'i Faith and Economics: A Review and Synthesis," *Baha'i Studies Review* 7 (1997), www.bahai-library.org/.

4. Parker Palmer, *The Active Life: A Spirituality of Work, Creativity and Caring* (San Francisco: Jossey-Bass, 1990), p. 44.

5. The Business News Luminaries: B.C. Forbes (www.newsluminaries.com/forbesbc.htm).

6. Alex Tizon, "Lean and Meaningful," *San Francisco Examiner*, October 22, 2000, p. J-1.

7. Stephen Overell, "Plain Dealing Pays Dividends," *The Financial Times*, August 22, 2000.

8. Jim Braham, "The Spiritual Side," *Industry Week*, February 1, 1999; and Shelley Donald Coolidge, "Corporate Decency Prevails at Malden Mills," *Christian Science Monitor*, March 28, 1996; and Helen Mintz Belitsky, "Portrait: Aaron Feuerstein—Flames and Light," *Hadassah Magazine* 77, no. 10 (June–July 1996).

9. Alex Tizon, "Lean and Meaningful," p. J-2; Alfie Kohn, *No Contest: The Case against Competition* (New York: Houghton Mifflin, 1986, 1992) and www.alfiekohn.org/; Jesper Isaksen, "Constructing Meaning in Repetitive Work," *Journal of Humanistic Psychology* 40, no. 3 (Summer 2000), pp. 85–107.

10. Paul Hawken, *Growing a Business* (New York: Fireside/Simon & Schuster, 1987), pp. 139–140.

11. Alfie Kohn, "In Pursuit of Affluence, at a High Price," *The New York Times on the Web*, National Science/Health, February 2, 1999, www.nytimes.com; and www.alfiekohn.org/; Scott Hauser, "Money? Thanks, But No Thanks," *Rochester Review* (University of Rochester) 62, no. 3 (Spring–Summer 2000); David G. Myers, "Wealth, Well-Being, and the New American Dream," Center for a New American Dream, April 2000 (www.newdream.org/discuss/myers.html).

12. Terrence Smith interviewing Marvin Kalb, *The NewsHour with Jim Lehrer*, November 8, 2000 (www.pbs.org/newshour/)

13. Steven Carter, *Civility* (New York: HarperCollins, 1998), pp. 116–117.

14. For additional information on meaning, see the International Network on Personal Meaning, Vancouver, British Columbia (www.meaning.ca).

15. Jacob Needleman, *Time and the Soul* (New York: Currency/Doubleday, 1998), p. 100.

16. Linda Manassee Buell, Simplify Life, Poway, CA (www.simplifylife.com).

17. Michael Lerner, *Spirit Matters* (Charlottesville, VA: Hampton Roads, 2000).

18. For more information about remote healing and prayer, see Larry Dossey, M.D., *Healing Words: The Power of Prayer and the Practice of Medicine* (New York: HarperCollins, 1997); and "Research Review," *Ways of the Healer* (Institute for Health and Healing of the California Pacific Medical Center in San Francisco) Winter–Spring 1999. For information about the effects of meditation on stress and health, see William Collinge, M.P.H., Ph.D., "Why Meditate? Because It's Good Medicine" (WebMD Health, www.webmd.com). For information about color psychology and prison aggression studies, see "Baker-Miller Pink," Color Matters, The Body (www.colormatters.com).

19. Deepak Chopra, M.D., *The Seven Spiritual Laws of Success* (Novato, CA: New World Library, 1994), pp. 32–33.

20. Lama Surya Das, *Awakening the Buddha Within: Tibeten Wisdom for the Western World* (New York: Broadway Books, 1997).

21. Lucia Capacchione, *Visioning: Ten Steps to Designing the Life of Your Dreams* (Boston: Shambhala, 2000).

Bibliography and Reading Guide

For easier reference, I've organized the following list by relevance to each Key—growth, vision, relationship and wisdom—though many of the books can be cross-referenced. You'll find additional books in the endnotes for each section. The suggested readings are intended to offer a variety of perspectives on each issue.

SECTION 1: THERE'S MORE THAN ONE WAY TO DEFINE GROWTH

Adrienne, Carol. *The Purpose of Your Life*. New York: Eagle Brook/William Morrow, 1998.

Block, Peter. *Stewardship: Choosing Service over Self-Interest*. San Francisco, Berrett-Koehler, 1993.

Hansen, Jeffrey A. *Surviving Success: Managing the Challenges of Growth*. Grants Pass, OR: Oasis Press/PSI Research, 1998.

Harman, Willis, and Maya Porter. *The New Business of Business: Sharing Responsibility for a Positive Global Future*. San Francisco: Berrett-Koehler, 1997.

Havel, Vaclav. *The Art of the Impossible: Politics as Morality in Practice*. New York: Fromm International, 1998.

Havel, Vaclav. *Open Letters: Selected Writings, 1965–1990*. New York: Vintage Books, Random House, 1992.

Hawken, Paul. *Growing a Business*. New York: Fireside/Simon & Schuster, 1987.

Korten, David C. *The Post-Corporate World: Life after Capitalism*. West Hartford, CT: Kumerian Press; San Francisco: Berrett-Koehler, 1999.

Korten, David C. *When Corporations Rule the World*. West Hartford, CT: Kumerian Press; San Francisco: Berrett-Koehler, 1995, 1996.

Parker J. *Let Your Life Speak: Listening for the Voice of Vocation.* San Francisco: Jossey-Bass, 2000.

Palmer, Parker J. *The Active Life: A Spirituality of Work, Creativity and Caring.* San Francisco: Jossey-Bass, 1990.

Peterman, John. "The Rise and Fall of the J. Peterman Company." *Harvard Business Review,* September–October 1999, pp. 59–66 (Reprint no. 99507).

Petzinger, Thomas, Jr. *The New Pioneers: The Men and Women Who Are Transforming the Workplace and Marketplace.* New York: Simon & Schuster, 1999.

Pierce, Linda Breen. *Choosing Simplicity: Real People Finding Peace and Fulfillment in a Complex World.* Carmel, CA: Gallagher Press, 2000.

Richards, Dick. *Artful Work: Awakening Joy, Meaning and Commitment in the Workplace.* New York: Berkeley Books, 1995.

Schumacher, E. F. *Small Is Beautiful: Economics as If People Mattered.* New York: Harper & Rowe, 1973.

Senge, Peter. *The Dance of Change: The Challenges to Sustaining Momentum in Learning Organizations.* New York: Currency/Doubleday, 1999.

Toms, Justine Willis, and Michael Toms. *True Work: The Sacred Dimension of Earning a Living.* New York: Bell Tower, 1998.

Whitmyer, Claude. *Mindfulness and Meaningful Work: Explorations of Right Livelihood.* Berkeley, CA: Parallax Press, 1994.

Whyte, David. *The Heart Aroused: Poetry and the Preservation of the Soul in Corporate America.* New York: Currency/Doubleday, 1994.

SECTION 2: TO LIVE LARGE, YOU HAVE TO VISION BIG

Allen, Marc. *Visionary Business: An Entrepreneur's Guide to Success.* Novato, CA: New World Library, 1995.

Buzan, Tony. *The Mind Map Book: How to Use Radiant Thinking to Maximize Your Brain's Untapped Potential.* New York: Dutton/Penguin Books, 1993.

Capacchione, Lucia. *Visioning: Ten Steps to Designing the Life of Your Dreams.* Boston: Shambhala, 2000.

Claxton, Guy. *Hare Brain, Tortoise Mind: How Intelligence Increases When You Think Less.* New York: Ecco Press/HarperPerennial, 1997.

Cooperrider, David, et al. *Appreciative Inquiry: Rethinking Human Organization toward a Positive Theory of Change.* Champaign, IL: Stipes, 2000.

Ellinor, Linda and Glenna Gerard. *Dialogue: Rediscover the Transforming Power of Conversation.* New York: John Wiley & Sons, 1998.

Foster, Jack. *Ideaship: How to Get Ideas Flowing in Your Workplace.* San Francisco: Berrett-Koehler 2001.

Hall, Stacey, and Jan Brogniez. *Attracting Perfect Customers: The Power of Strategic Synchronicity.* San Francisco: Berrett-Koehler, 2001.

Jones, Laurie Beth. *The Path: Creating Your Mission Statement for Work and for Life.* New York: Hyperion, 1996.

Ludy, Perry. *Profit Building: Cutting Costs without Cutting Profit.* San Francisco: Berrett-Koehler, 2000.

Nair, Keshavan. *A Higher Standard of Leadership: Lessons from the Life of Gandhi.* San Francisco: Berrett-Koehler, 1994, 1997.

Rosen, Robert H., Ph.D. *The Healthy Company: Eight Strategies to Develop People, Productivity and Profits.* New York: G. P. Putnam's Sons, 1991.

Wheatley, Margaret. *Turning to One Another: Simple Conversations to Restore Hope to the Future.* San Francisco: Berrett-Koehler, 2002.

SECTION 3: RIGHT RELATIONSHIP IS A BIG-VISION CRAFT

Baron, Renee, and Elizabeth Wagele. *The Enneagram Made Easy.* New York: HarperCollins, 1994.

Behr, E. Thomas, Ph.D. *The Tao of Sales: The Easy Way to Sell in Tough Times.* Rockport, MA: Element Books, 1997.

Carnegie, Dale. *How to Win Friends and Influence People.* New York: Pocket Books/Simon & Schuster, 1936.

Chambers, Harry E. *The Bad Attitude Survival Guide.* Reading, MA: Addison-Wesley, 1998.

Chappell, Tom. *The Soul of a Business: Managing for Profit and the Common Good.* New York: Bantam Books, 1993.

Garfield, Charles, Cindy Spring, and Sedonia Cahill. *Wisdom Circles: A Guide to Self-Discovery and Community Building in Small Groups.* New York: Hyperion, 1998.

Garrett, J. T., and Michael Tlanusta Garrett. *Medicine of the Cherokee: The Way of Right Relationship.* Santa Fe, NM: Bear & Co., 1996.

Gozdz, Kazimierz. *Community Building: Renewing Spirit and Learning in Business.* San Francisco: New Leaders Press/Sterling & Stone, 1995.

Heider, John. *The Tao of Leadership.* Atlanta: Humanics New Age, 1985.

Myers, Esabel Briggs, with Peter B. Myers. *Gifts Differing: Understanding Personality Type.* Palo Alto, CA: Davies-Black Publishing, 1980, 1995.

Riso, Don Richard. *Understanding the Enneagram: The Practical Guide to Personality Types.* Boston: Houghton Mifflin Company, 1990.

Riso, Don Richard, and Ross Hudson. *The Wisdom of the Enneagram: The Complete Guide to Psychological and Spiritual Growth for the Nine Personality Types.* New York: Bantam Books, 1999.

Shafir, Rebecca Z. *The Zen of Listening: Mindful Communication in the Age of Distraction.* Wheaton, IL: Quest Books, 2000.

Walters, Jamie. Ivy Sea Online Communication & Leadership Center. Ivy Sea, Inc., San Francisco, c. 1997–2001; www.ivysea.com/

SECTION 4: TO LIVE FROM THE SOURCE, REPLENISH THE WELL

Das, Lama Surya. *Awakening the Buddha Within: Tibeten Wisdom for the Western World.* New York: Broadway Books, 1997.

Donald, David Herbert. *Lincoln.* New York: Simon & Schuster, 1995.

Fontana, David, Ph.D. *Learn to Meditate: A Practical Guide to Self-Discovery and Fulfillment.* San Francisco: Chronicle Books/Duncan Baird Publishers, 1999.

Forstater, Mark. *The Spiritual Teachings of Marcus Aurelius.* New York: HarperCollins, 2000.

Fox, Matthew. *The Reinvention of Work: A New Vision of Livelihood for Our Time.* New York: HarperSanFrancisco, HarperCollins, 1994.

Frankl, Victor. *Man's Search for Meaning.* New York: Washington Square Press/Pocket Books, 1959, 1984.

George, Mike. *Learn to Relax: A Practical Guide to Easing Tension & Conquering Stress.* San Francisco: Chronicle Books/Duncan Baird, 1998.

Hall, Donald. *Life Work.* Boston: Beacon Press, 1993.

Hamill, Pete. *The Subway Series Reader.* New York: Simon & Schuster, 2000.

Harvey, Andrew. *The Direct Path: Creating a Journey to the Divine Using the World's Great Mystical Traditions.* New York: Broadway Books, 2000.

Harvey, Andrew. *Son of Man: The Mystical Path to Christ.* New York: Tarcher/Putnam, 1998.

Ingram, Catherine. *In the Footsteps of Gandhi: Conversations with Spiritual Social Activists.* Berkeley, CA: Parallax Press, 1990.

Kohn, Alfie. *No Contest: The Case against Competition.* New York: Houghton Mifflin, 1986, 1992. www.alfiekohn.org/

Kübler Ross, Elisabeth, and David Kessler. *Life Lessons.* New York: Scribners, 2000.

Kübler Ross, Elisabeth. *The Wheel of Life: A Memoir of Living and Dying.* New York: Scribners, 1997.

Lame Deer, John (Fire), and Richard Erdoes. *Lame Deer: Seeker of Visions.* New York: Simon & Schuster, 1972.

Leider, Richard J. and David A. Shapiro. *Whistle While You Work: Heeding Your Life's Calling.* San Francisco: Berrett-Koehler, 2001.

Lerner, Michael. *Spirit Matters.* Charlottesville, VA: Hampton Roads, 2000.

Mitchell, Stephen, ed. and trans. *Tao Te Ching*. New York: Harper & Row, 1988.

Mitchell, Stephen. *A Book of Psalms*. New York: HarperCollins, 1993.

Morgan, Sharon Drew. *Selling with Integrity: Reinventing Sales through Collaboration, Respect, and Serving*. San Francisco: Berrett-Koehler, 1997.

Muller, Wayne. *Sabbath: Finding Rest, Renewal, and Delight in Our Busy Lives*. New York: Bantam Books, 1999.

Needleman, Jacob. *Money and the Meaning of Life*. New York: Currency/Doubleday, 1991.

Needleman, Jacob. *Time and the Soul*. New York: Currency/Doubleday, 1998.

Orman, Suze. *The Courage to Be Rich: Creating a Life of Material and Spiritual Abundance*. New York: Riverhead Books/Penguin Putnam, 1999.

Richmond, Lewis. *Work as a Spiritual Practice*. New York: Broadway Books, 1999.

Rohr, Richard, and Andreas Ebert. *Discovering the Enneagram: An Ancient Tool for a New Spiritual Journey*. New York: Crossroad, 1997.

Robbins, Anthony. *Personal Power II: The Driving Force*. San Diego, CA: Robbins Research International, Inc., 1993, 1996.

Roland, Paul. *Revelations: Wisdom of the Ages*. Berkeley, CA: Ulysses Press, 1995.

Staniforth, Maxwell, trans. *Marcus Aurelius Meditations*. New York: Penguin Classics, PenguinPutnam, 1964.

White Eagle. *The Quiet Mind*. Hampshire, England: White Eagle Publishing Trust, 1972; 15th impression, 1994.

SELECT INTERNET RESOURCES

About.com: www.about.com

American Independent Business Alliance: www.reclaimdemocracy.org

Berrett-Koehler Publishers, Inc.: www.bkpub.com

Business Alliance for Local Living Economies: www.livingeconomies.org

Center for Small Business and the Environment: www.geocities.com/aboutcsbe/

CEO Refresher: www.refresher.com/ceo.html

Cyber-Nation Quotations Database: www.cyber-nation.com

Inc.com: www.inc.com

Ivy Sea Online Leadership & Communication Center: www.ivysea.com

Simplify Life: www.simplifylife.com

U.S. Neighbor: http://www.usneighbor.org/

Working Solo, Inc.: www.workingsolo.com

Hope Magazine, Brookline, Maine: www.hopemag.com

Index

About the Author

The daughter of self-employed parents, Jamie Walters launched her San Francisco–based consulting firm in 1992. Since then, Ivy Sea, Inc., has provided innovative leadership, communication, and systems counsel to a wide variety of organizations, large and small. In addition to being Ivy Sea's chief vision and strategy officer, Walters is the editor in chief and publisher of the firm's award-winning public-service Web site, Ivy Sea Online (www.ivysea.com). The site is an Inc.com content partner and has been recognized by Harvard Business School, CEO Refresher, Edu-Leadership.com, Entrepreneur's Edge, and others as one of the best sites on the Internet for small-business owners, entrepreneurs, and organizational leaders. Though Walters has written dozens of articles on leadership, organizational culture, communication, and mindset-management, *Big Vision, Small Business* is her first book. She lives in San Francisco with her husband and business partner, Tom Tshontikidis, and two cats, Uri and Josephine.

About Ivy Sea, Inc.

Ivy Sea, Inc., is a highly regarded "small size, big impact" organizational consulting firm based in San Francisco, California. The firm works with local, national, and international organizations to help foster new levels of inspiration and effectiveness in organizational leadership, culture, and communication. To that end, the group has supported such organizations as Agilent Technologies,

Banana Republic, California Federal Bank, Charles Schwab & Co., Gap Inc., St. Joseph's Healthcare System, Kaiser Permanente, Mervyns, and Chevron, as well as a variety of smaller enterprises and nonprofit organizations. In addition to its consulting services, Ivy Sea, Inc., publishes the award-winning Web portal, Ivy Sea Online (www.ivysea.com).

Berrett-Koehler Publishers

BERRETT-KOEHLER is an independent publisher of books, periodicals, and other publications at the leading edge of new thinking and innovative practice on work, business, management, leadership, stewardship, career development, human resources, entrepreneurship, and global sustainability.

Since the company's founding in 1992, we have been committed to supporting the movement toward a more enlightened world of work by publishing books, periodicals, and other publications that help us to integrate our values with our work and work lives, and to create more humane and effective organizations.

We have chosen to focus on the areas of work, business, and organizations, because these are central elements in many people's lives today. Furthermore, the work world is going through tumultuous changes, from the decline of job security to the rise of new structures for organizing people and work. We believe that change is needed at all levels—individual, organizational, community, and global—and our publications address each of these levels.

We seek to create new lenses for understanding organizations, to legitimize topics that people care deeply about but that current business orthodoxy censors or considers secondary to bottom-line concerns, and to uncover new meaning, means, and ends for our work and work lives.

See next pages for other publications
from Berrett-Koehler Publishers

101 Tips for Telecommuters
Successfully Manage Your Work, Team, Technology and Family

Debra A Dinnocenzo

101 Tips for Telecommuters tells you how to manage your time, balance telecommuting with family demands, and work effectively with others from afar, network the "virtual" way, get a grip on technological overkill, and even resist the ever-beckoning refrigerator when working at home! If you are one of the millions of Americans who wants to succeed in this exciting and challenging new way of work, let *101 Tips for Telecommuters* be your guide!

Paperback, 260 pages • ISBN 1-57675-069-8
Item #50698-415 $15.95

Bringing Your Soul to Work
An Everyday Practice

Cheryl Peppers and Alan Briskin

This new book addresses the gap between our inner lives and the work we do in the world. Case studies, personal stories, inspirational quotes, reflective questions, and concrete applications navigate readers through the real and troubling questions inherent in the workplace.

Paperback, 260 pages • ISBN 1-57675-111-2
Item #51112-415 $16.95

The Knowledge Engine
How to Create Fast Cycles of Knowledge-to-Performance and Performance-to-Knowledge

Lloyd Baird and John C. Henderson

The Knowledge Engine shows that in the new economy, knowledge must be captured from performance as it is happening and used to improve the next round of performance, integrating learning and performance into a continuous cycle. The authors show how to produce knowledge as part of the work process and quickly apply that learning back to performance to create a "knowledge engine" that drives ongoing performance improvement and adds value in every area of your organization.

Hardcover, 200 pages • ISBN 1-57675-104-X
Item #5104X-415 $27.95

Berrett-Koehler Publishers
PO Box 565, Williston, VT 05495-9900
Call toll-free! **800-929-2929** 7 am-9 pm Eastern Standard Time
Or fax your order to 802-864-7627
For fastest service order online: **www.bkconnection.com**